Optimizing Early Auditory Development for Communication and Education

This important resource offers teachers, parents, and medical professionals developmentally appropriate, easy-to-implement activities for developing and supporting a strong auditory foundation in young children, helping increase the depth and stability of children's auditory skills for future communication, language, and literacy learning opportunities. The book addresses specific areas of auditory processing – like decoding, organization, and prosodic – by defining the area and then providing strategies that can be integrated into any early childhood curriculum, home, and classroom environments. Comprehensive in scope, the book explores brain development specific to auditory processing and language and explains the connections between various aspects of auditory processing and its broader implications, including literacy. Addressing existing developmental gaps, this book is important reading for any early childhood educator and parents, as well as occupational therapists, speech-language pathologists, audiologists, pediatricians, educators and administrators, and school psychologists.

Kimberly A. Boynton is a certified speech-language pathologist with licenses in the areas of Speech Language Pathology, Director of Exceptional Services, and School Superintendent. She holds a Ph.D. in Educational Administration. She is currently the Coalition Director of Building Strong Brains, Elkhart County's Early Childhood Initiative, housed at the Community Foundation of Elkhart County, in Elkhart, Indiana.

Darah J. Regal is a certified audiologist who has specialized in auditory processing during her career as a university professor, clinical and educational audiologist, and as a parent. She holds a doctorate degree in audiology and is currently providing audiological services with Goshen Physicians, ENT, Speech and Audiology, Goshen, Indiana.

Optimizing Early Auditory Development for Communication and Education

Strategies for Ages 0–8

Kimberly A. Boynton and Darah J. Regal

Routledge
Taylor & Francis Group

NEW YORK AND LONDON

Designed cover image: Getty Images

First published 2025
by Routledge
605 Third Avenue, New York, NY 10158

and by Routledge
4 Park Square, Milton Park, Abingdon, Oxon, OX14 4RN

Routledge is an imprint of the Taylor & Francis Group, an informa business

© 2025 Taylor & Francis

The right of Kimberly A. Boynton and Darah J. Regal to be identified as authors of this work has been asserted in accordance with sections 77 and 78 of the Copyright, Designs and Patents Act 1988.

ISBN: 9781032647081 (hbk)
ISBN: 9781032634005 (pbk)
ISBN: 9781032647098 (ebk)

DOI: 10.4324/9781032647098

Typeset in Palatino
by KnowledgeWorks Global Ltd.

To my husband and best friend, Chris, a heartfelt thank you – your ongoing support of my personal and professional growth is unwavering, even when it means endless hours of researching, writing, reading, and working. You continue to value my love of learning and provide me with endless opportunities for laughter and joy in my life.

—Kimberly A. Boynton

The book is lovingly dedicated to my grandson, Emil. What a blessing you are in our lives. Grandma and Grandpa love you dearly and cherish the moments we share with you.

—Darah J. Regal

Contents

Meet the Authors

Dr. Kimberly A. Boynton is a certified Speech Language Pathologist holding the ASHA Certificate of Clinical Competence, Indiana Professional Licensing Agency Speech-Language Pathologist license, Indiana Department of Education licensing in the areas of Speech Language Pathology, Director of Exceptional Services, and School Superintendent. She has speech-language pathology experience working with children ages birth to high school in various early childhood education settings, public and private schools, home-based services, private practice, and clinical settings. She received a Bachelor of Science degree in Audiological and Speech Sciences and a Master of Science degree in Speech Language Pathology from Purdue University. She received her Director of Exceptional Learner's License from Ball State University. She received her Doctor of Philosophy degree in Educational Administration from Indiana State University. Dr. Boynton has held clinical and administrative positions in the field of education, an academic faculty position in higher education, and currently serves in a leadership role supporting early childhood collective impact work in Elkhart, Indiana. She has focused her work in the area of high-quality early childhood services and community supports for young children and families, including significant work on community-level committees and task force groups to support and empower children and families. School-based experience has focused on the provision of speech and language assessment and intervention services, educator professional development, teacher evaluation system implementation, grant writing and management, and development and implementation of early childhood services. Dr. Boynton worked as a Director of Early Childhood Services within a large urban public school district in Northern Indiana working collaboratively with community early childhood programs and Head Start. Additionally, she studied and led the implementation of early childhood programming to support the community's need for additional early childhood opportunities for children and families. She has held the position of Coordinator of Early Childhood/Preschool Special Education working to ensure equitable and appropriate services for children. She has worked as an Assistant Professor of Speech Language Pathology, teaching, serving, and conducting research. She has taught undergraduate and graduate speech-language pathology courses in the areas of speech and language development, assessment, and intervention, and provided clinical practicum supervision to graduate students. Dr. Boynton is the author of *Job Satisfaction of School-Based Speech-Language Pathologists: Insights to Inform Effective Educational Leadership* and *Supporting Early Speech-Language Development: Strategies for Ages 0-8*. Dr. Boynton's current work provides the opportunity to work collectively with partners and stakeholders in Elkhart County to shift the early childhood system in the areas of maternal and child health, quality child care and early learning environments, and community supports for children and families, to ensure young children and families are prepared and have the support needed to learn and thrive.

Dr. Darah J. Regal is a certified audiologist with a passion for auditory processing as a professional, educator, family member, and parent. During her career, she has worked with birth through geriatric patients providing diagnostic and rehabilitative audiology services. As an educational audiologist in Elkins, WV, she was asked to develop

an auditory processing evaluation protocol by the special education director and speech-language pathologists. Working with an amazing group of speech-language pathologists, she valued the collaborative environment that resulted in significant improvement for the children they served. As she became more proficient at auditory processing evaluations, she researched and developed recommendations for technology support, therapy interventions, and classroom management. She will forever be grateful to the speech-language pathologists at Randolph County Schools who encouraged, facilitated, and developed strong therapy interventions for preschool through high school students with auditory processing deficits.

As an assistant professor of audiology at Andrews University, she developed, marketed, and refined a successful auditory processing protocol and remediation program in cooperation with area speech-language pathologists. In addition, her students learned how to develop and implement therapy programs designed to help children and adults improve auditory processing skills for literacy, academic success, and communication. Twenty years in an academic setting provided opportunities for collaboration, research, continuing education, and further development of specified auditory processing interventions dependent on the area of auditory processing that needed to be strengthened. When learning about auditory processing in classes, she had students who recognized their own challenges with processing auditory information. She was able to work with students who struggled in university classes and provide strategies and recommendations for better educational success. Dr. Kim Boynton, co-author of this book, was one of the speech-language pathologists who came to the university to observe an auditory processing evaluation and has demonstrated a gift for developing auditory processing strategies and successful remediations. Dr. Regal has learned so much from collaborating with speech-language pathologists, especially Dr. Kim Boynton, Barbara "Bobbi" Trimboli, Pam Dutcher, and Lara Scheidler-Smith, strengthening her belief that collaboration is so valuable. In addition, while teaching at the university, she had the opportunity to work with so many future audiologists and speech-language pathologists, many of whom have expanded and continued to provide auditory processing evaluations and remediations/therapies.

The current phase of her career has been working within a medical environment, again starting an auditory processing program for an organization in the area that has never offered this service. She has been so blessed with supportive otolaryngologists (ENT) and administrators who see the value in diagnosing and remediating auditory processing disorders.

As a family member, she experienced the significant effect a traumatic brain injury can have on the family after her older brother, Fred, was hit by a car while riding a bicycle. MRIs, CT scans were not available yet, and special education and/or IEPs had not been implemented in the 1970s. The family devoted themselves to helping her brother; reading all his textbooks to him (he had a phenomenal memory, if you read it to him, he remembered it), building a treehouse, facilitating mechanical skills, financially providing for tutors and speech pathology, advocating with teachers and administrators, and so much more. They knew he was still intelligent but not able to read/learn like typical children. Her parents rejected the suggestions from educators to take him out of school because he couldn't read. Remember – No special education in the 1970s. Fred graduated from college and has had a successful career as a registered nurse.

The example of her parents and professionals who worked with Fred, especially Mr. Glen McDermott, speech pathologist, inspired her to want to make a positive difference for other families. She developed a mindset that the brain is moldable, even after injury, so – never give up, keep looking for solutions, have faith, and pray for guidance.

As a parent, she developed strategies to work with her own children who had auditory processing deficits. During this phase, she realized the limited resources for parents and out of necessity began to develop games/ideas/therapies for helping her own children "rewire" for education expectations. She personally felt the frustration of auditory processing deficits not being recognized as a special education category by the state for accommodations within the classroom. For several years, she and her husband, Jeff, also an audiologist, worked with their own children in the evenings, hired tutors, and found effective remediations. Her journey as a parent was challenging but eventually very rewarding as she was able to see her children succeed, graduate from college, graduate school, and work as co-professionals. She made mistakes, there were tears of frustration, and arguments. There were also successes, laughter, and confidence building. She developed a deep sense of empathy for parents on similar journeys. She understands the challenge and wants to encourage parents and educators that the children are worth the effort. The brain for most children can be strengthened/wired/rewired. They can develop auditory processing skills for success. Oh, how she wishes there would have been a book like this when her children were young!

Her greatest hope is for parents, educators, and health professionals to work toward developing auditory processing skills when children are young. She believes early intervention is vital for developing ear-brain connections for communication and education. She wants parents to feel empowered to help their child at home in fun engaging ways to facilitate auditory skills for future academic and communication needs.

Preface

The concept of this book grew out of too many collaborative referrals to count, hundreds of opportunities to brainstorm and problem-solve, and a strong commitment to understand how we could work together as a speech-language pathologist and audiologist, to support children with auditory processing and language challenges thrive and reach their goals. Our "why" is a determination to continue to build awareness of the importance of supporting the development of auditory and language systems during the early years to ensure opportunities for children to develop strong communication and cognitive systems. Our work with children and families in the fields of speech-language pathology and audiology has taught us the importance of these systems in daily communication, interactions, learning, and social experiences. The goal of this book isn't to provide all the answers, but we are confident that providing opportunities for auditory and language learning through interactions and experiences during the critical early childhood years will support a positive path forward on a child's individual learning journey.

We hope you will travel with us through this book to learn more about ways to support the development and strengthening of a young child's auditory and language systems. If you know a child who is experiencing challenges listening, attending, expressing thoughts and ideas, we hope this book will provide strategies and ideas for seeking support. Lastly, we hope that you will find information within these pages that resonates with you, causes you to pause, and considers the impact of auditory and language use and processing in our daily lives, or perhaps, sparks your curiosity to learn more about these areas of development. We hope to empower you with ideas that are practical and can be incorporated in your daily routines at home and in the classroom. The auditory, speech, and language systems can be strengthened and new ways to process are possible. We look forward to walking this auditory and language learning journey together with you!

We want to thank all the children and families that have invited us into their lives – family members, friends, and clients. We have learned so much from you and you inspire us to continue learning, building awareness, and exploring innovative ways to support the acquisition, development, and use of the auditory and language systems for communication, learning, and interacting. Thank you for always reminding us that development and learning can and should be fun!

Acknowledgments

Kimberly A. Boynton

I want to express my sincere appreciation to my colleague and dear friend, Dr. Darah Regal. You have inspired me, challenged me, and shared your expertise with me for over two decades. I am truly a better speech-language pathologist because you helped me embrace an understanding of the impact of auditory processing on communication, learning, interactions, motivation, and confidence. You have taught me more than I can convey in words, and you motivate me to continue to learn and grow as a speech-language pathologist. I am thankful that we have walked the journey of writing this book together because it has offered the opportunity to laugh, learn, and brainstorm together, challenging us to learn and grow in collaboration, determination, and motivation. You have provided answers, hope, and opportunities to so many children and families. I have been humbled to be part of this ongoing collaboration. I am honored to know you, learn from you, and to call you a friend.

Thank you to everyone at Routledge Taylor & Francis Group, including the editors, copyeditors, and all who shared in the work. Thank you to Alexis and Justin at Taylor & Francis who answered all our questions and helped make this book a reality with their guidance, insight, and intentional feedback.

I want to thank all the children and families who have invited me into their lives – whether family, friends, or clients, I always enjoy the opportunity to use language and auditory processing to communicate and interact. Thank you to all the children and families who have joined in the many language development and learning opportunities. You have given me a precious gift, learning from the true experts – parents, caregivers, and children.

I have endless appreciation for the talented and committed early childhood professionals I have worked alongside over the years. I always think about all the early learning opportunities, interactions, and experiences that are shared during the early years. I am confident these valuable moments and experiences have resulted in wonderful growth and learning in children's lives. The work you do daily is so important to a child's early development. I continue to learn so many lessons from the work you do and the interactions we have. Thank you for sharing your expertise and love of early childhood with me.

I am forever grateful for all the talented and committed community partners and stakeholders currently engaged in the Building Strong Brains, Elkhart County's Early Childhood Initiative, work. I continue to learn daily from all of you about the impact of collectively working to shift a system. We continue to be challenged in new ways, are encouraged to think differently, and strive for transformational change to improve outcomes for young children and families in Elkhart County. I am thankful for your shared time, expertise, and innovative thinking. Together, the community is working to ensure all young children in Elkhart County are *born to thrive*!

As I take each new step on my personal and professional journey, I will always recognize and honor the commitment of my parents, George Weil and the late Mary Weil, who encouraged me to ask questions, search for answers, care for others, and to never stop learning and growing.

I continue to find true joy in my interactions with two very important children in my life, Isabelle Marie and Carter Julius. My niece and nephew bring joy, inspiration, and a strong motivation for me to work to ensure auditory and language learning experiences for all children. I continue to learn so much from them with each opportunity, going on an adventure, playing, spending time at the park, and talking on the phone. Sharing in their ongoing inquisitive thinking, care for others, and enthusiasm for learning, with a new focus on learning to read, is evidence of the value of early auditory and language experiences. I look forward to continuing to support their interests, curiosity, and creativity, in ways that are meaningful to them, as they continue to learn and grow. Being their Aunt Kim will always be one of my most cherished experiences.

Finally, but most importantly, a heartfelt thank you to my husband, Chris, who offers endless encouragement and support in all my personal and professional endeavors. Thank you for sharing in my joy, offering the needed support when I fail forward, and being a true partner on our life journey together.

Darah J. Regal

Thank you is not enough to express my gratitude to Dr. Kim Boynton for inviting me on the journey to write this book. You have continued to inspire me to find answers to questions, research possibilities, and collaborate on challenging cases. Our professional collaboration has led to a valued friendship. You have provided cheers for my successes, a listening ear on my tough days, and continued encouragement professionally. On more occasions than I can count, I have been inspired by the positive impact you have had on people's lives. As I have read the book through all the stages from rough draft to completion, I have been amazed at your ability to bring ideas to life through your vivid, thoughtful, practical writing style. Thank you for your patience as I wrote, jotted down, or texted ideas. I am forever grateful for your ability to organize our notes, ideas, and combine audiology and speech pathology perspectives into a useful guide for parents, educators, and health professionals. You are a wonderful mentor, guiding me through this process, with unbounded kindness, patience, and positive comments.

A special thank you to my children, Daniel and David, who have provided love, laughter, inspiration, and determination to find solutions. Thank you for your continued willingness to try new techniques, explore possibilities, and for your hard work to increase your own auditory processing skills. You both continue to inspire me as co-professionals. Daniel, you are an amazing speech-language pathologist naturally embedding your creativity, musical talent, and language skills to help families with young children develop speech, language, and auditory skills. David, you are a talented audiologist providing diagnostic and rehabilitative services, as well as teaching and marketing skills with a sharp business mind. Thank you both for your willingness to share your expertise with me about areas of the professions where your knowledge exceeds mine. Thank you, Ashley, for listening to ideas and helping with design and content. Thank you, Daniel and Ashley, for being amazing parents to Emil, and using so many of the techniques in this book to strengthen auditory skills.

Thank you, Elizabeth Bame, for sharing your artistic skills for the illustrations. Even though I struggled sometimes to use words to describe the outcome I desired, you patiently continued to revamp and recreate illustrations that were clear, concise, and approachable. The ideas in my head are now visible through your artistic talent – thank you!

Thank you to my parents, Phillip and Jean, and siblings, Martha and Fred, who provided the initial spark of inspiration and passion for the brain and its ability to rewire and facilitate learning. Although it was a difficult journey, your perseverance and determination gave me a strong example of what it takes to find a positive outcome from a seemingly impossible situation. Never give up, keep learning, growing, and having faith. You provided a Christian example and instilled a deep trust in the power of prayer.

Thank you to my many students who listened, applied knowledge, and are now facilitating and building auditory and language processing skills for so many families. Special thank you to all my student researchers who worked countless hours together with me to find answers. I loved teaching and drawing positive energy from the classroom setting. Thank you for working with me to help the families that entrusted their loved ones to us for auditory processing evaluations and therapy. Every story was different, with common threads and unique personalities and abilities.

Dr. David Sabato and Dr. Savita Collins, thank you for your immediate support and encouragement to provide auditory processing testing in the ENT/Audiology clinic. Dr. Sabato, thank you for your positive attitude, love for people, undaunted passion for surgical intervention even for challenging cases, appreciation for audiology, encouragement to "teach" within the clinical setting, and for your ability to always stretch me professionally to be the best I can be. Dr. Collins, thank you for your professional support of auditory processing and for valuing audiology input for best patient care. Your deep commitment to best practice, personalized patient care, and a continual desire to be an excellent, caring provider for your patients is inspiring. You are both amazing ENTs and I have been very blessed to work with you.

Special acknowledgment to the audiologists and professionals specializing in auditory processing who have educated and challenged me on my professional journey. Dr. Stephen Prescod, Dr. Thomas Hemeyer, Dr. Jack Katz, Dr. Deborah Moncrieff, Dr. Robert Keith, Dr. Frank Musiek, Dr. Terri Bellis, and Dr. Nina Kraus, thank you for your research, expertise, and willingness to share your knowledge. All of you have provided resources that have shaped my auditory processing protocols and remediation strategies. Your research, creativity, discoveries, and professional development have benefitted countless families, including my own. Thank you for being willing to share your expertise, I am grateful.

To my husband and best friend, Jeff. Thank you for all the laughter, love, and professional collaboration. Thank you for listening and discussing audiology, I'm grateful to have a great husband who is also an amazing audiologist. You have been there through school, work, family, laughter, tears, triumphs, and hard times with a shoulder to cry on, an ear for listening, laughter to lighten the mood, and sometimes a push of encouragement to keep me moving forward.

1

Introduction to the Auditory Processing System

The concept of this book grew out of the collegial and collaborative work of two colleagues, who value the connection and alignment of the work of audiologists and speech-language pathologists. Although the work of audiologists focuses on the prevention, assessment, and treatment of hearing and balance, and speech-language pathologists focus on speech, language, voice, cognition, feeding, and swallowing, there are obvious and important collaborative connections between these areas of practice. As colleagues, we have continued to develop a deeper understanding and appreciation for this collaboration, with the goal of supporting young children and their families.

More specifically, our friendship and ongoing collaborative work together grew out of a strong determination to provide comprehensive assessment and effective intervention for children with auditory processing deficits. Our continued dialogue, sharing of resources, challenging each other with difficult and complex questions, and the strong desire to support the needs of children with auditory processing and language deficits supported our realization that when considering auditory processing and language development, there is no better place to begin than during the critical early childhood years. We believe there is a significant opportunity to enrich the development of

DOI: 10.4324/9781032647098-1

young children by providing intentional, consistent, and ongoing auditory and language opportunities during the early years.

Research has provided evidence of the significance of the critical developmental period, spanning birth to eight years. These early years serve a critical role in the language, motor, social-emotional, and cognitive development of a young child (Tierney & Nelson, 2009). The early years of a child's life offer an opportunity to provide rich developmental and learning experiences during a time when the brain has increased plasticity and responsiveness to developing neural connections. In fact, the brain architecture needed for a child's future learning and development is impacted by a young child's early experiences. During the early years of a child's development, their brain develops neural connections between neurons, supporting their present and future learning. Development during an infant's earliest months and years results in at least 1 million new neural connections each second, more than at any other time during their life (Center on the Developing Child, 2007). In fact, the developmental period between birth and age three is a critical period for brain development, providing an important opportunity to ensure nurturing and responsive experiences during the young child's daily routines and interactions.

The evidence that identifies the significance of providing developmental experiences, opportunities, and responsive interactions aligns with the importance of recognizing the potential for enhancing auditory development for future learning and interactions. While we know you are likely already engaging in meaningful activities supporting auditory and language development with children in your lives, we hope this book will allow you to recognize the significance of the engagement in these activities, recognize the benefits of incorporating these opportunities into a young child's daily routines and interactions, and perhaps explore additional or novel ways to continue to support building strong auditory and language foundations.

The authors of this book have worked with many children in clinical practice, in a variety of settings, including schools, clinics, healthcare, and private practice over the years. While our work has encompassed a broad scope of practice, working with individuals with diverse hearing, speech, and language needs, we have continued to explore and strengthen our collaborative work in supporting individuals with auditory processing and language deficits and disorders. In continuing this ongoing exploration, we have developed an increased interest in considering ways to support early auditory and language development during the critical early childhood years as a means of prevention and early intervention. We hope you will join us in the exploration of the complexity of processing auditory and language information, recognizing the impact on daily interactions, routines, and tasks. As we progress on the journey of this book, you will find **Auditory Amplifiers** along the way, providing opportunities for reflection, connections to real-life experiences, discussion prompts, and considerations of the content and context of the importance of developing strong auditory processing and language systems. We hope you find these momentary pauses helpful in navigating this book and the included information, examples, and strategies. We hope that you will identify and celebrate ways you are already supporting the auditory and language development of young children in your life. Whether you are a parent, grandparent, extended family member, friend, caregiver, or early childhood professional, thank you for your ongoing commitment to sharing in the learning and interactions of the young children in your life. The early childhood years are full of joyful and fun opportunities to learn and grow together!

We have worked with many children and their families over the years, each unique in their strengths, needs, and goals. We are humbled by these families who are often frustrated, concerned, worried, but determined to support their child's success. These amazingly talented and enthusiastic children and their families exhibit tenacity, resilience, determination, and grit to succeed in school, social interactions, and life situations. Parents, caregivers, and in many cases their children can articulate what the challenges are. They often know the "what" but are frustrated because they don't understand the "why." In some cases, the frustration has deep roots developed by years of frustration, avoidance of social interactions, or feelings of failure. While in many cases, there are challenges, frustrations, and at times feelings of defeat, we have found hope in the identification of the specific auditory skill deficit, the ability to define an intervention uniquely targeting that skill, and the moments of success that are realized. In fact, for some families, simply hearing affirmation of a reason for the difficulty with processing auditory and language information brings a sense of relief. Knowing the root cause offers an opportunity to take intentional and focused action.

Learning from the Experts: Children and Families

For children with auditory processing deficits, daily social interactions, auditory, reading, and writing tasks may be difficult in isolation or collectively, but we have discovered that these children often assume that everyone uses an increased amount of effort to achieve daily tasks and routines. We encourage you to pause and consider this for a moment. Imagine if each auditory or language task in your daily interactions and activities required the same level of focus, determination, and time to complete, from listening to your favorite audiobook, to recalling the two things your friend asked you to pick up at the grocery store, to solving a complex multistep math word problem. What if you simply assumed everyone put the same significant amount of effort into every auditory or language task completed each day? Recalling, decoding, organizing, responding, and discriminating speech and environmental sounds are all necessary components of processing and interacting with the auditory and language world around us. How exhausting might it be if we needed to use the same level of cognitive load and energy to process every auditory or language aspect of the world around us?

Let's continue this thinking as we consider a young child who needs to use focused attention for a full school day filled with multistep directions, integration of auditory, visual, and motor information, and language tasks with varying degrees of complexity. Growing evidence suggests a connection between hearing loss and fatigue. What if a child required an equal amount of attention and energy to complete each task during the school day? How might this child feel at the end of the day?

Growing evidence suggests a connection between hearing loss and fatigue. In fact, research indicates that listening can be challenging when hearing loss is a factor (Davis et al., 2021; Holman et al., 2021; Hornsby, 2013; Hornsby & Kipp, 2016; Hornsby et al., 2022; Lindburg et al., 2021). As we continue to explore the impact of increased focused attention for extended periods of time resulting from hearing loss, or in the case of our discussion, challenges with auditory processing are important to consider. In fact, research suggests that when mental fatigue is a factor resulting from sustained processing of auditory information, there are changes in brain activation that indicate a decrease in focused attention. Additionally, research suggests this brain activation is correlated to a decrease in motivation and engagement linked to mental fatigue (Moore et al., 2017).

It is not surprising that many of the children we have worked with over the years experience significant fatigue at the end of their school day, which in some cases results in avoidance of homework, decreased social interactions, demonstrating acting out behaviors, zoning out in front of the TV, or napping after school. It is important to note that as a child gets older and notices their peers understand with greater ease, quickly following directions and completing other auditory tasks, they will often begin to think there is something wrong with them. They may begin to wonder: Why can't I understand? Why do I need people to repeat what they said? It is important to recognize that with increased self-awareness, there can be a resulting negative impact on self-esteem, confidence, and a willingness to attempt novel, challenging, or complex tasks. The impact of auditory processing deficits expands beyond missing all the presented directions, experiencing difficulties with social interactions, or answering a question with a related, but incorrect response. We will explore the task-related impact, but it is also important to discuss the impact on a child's motivation and confidence.

With the purpose of this book outlined, let's begin our exploration of the complexity of the auditory system, the areas of auditory processing, and language learning. As we process auditory and language information daily, we may not pause to consider the complexity of decoding, organizing, and integrating needed to effectively and efficiently process in our environment.

Processing Environmental Information

Although you may not pause to consider the complexity of the auditory system daily, we are going to invite you to travel a journey with us as we highlight important components of the auditory system and the way it works to support effective and efficient processing of auditory information. As we begin considering the auditory system, it is important to note that there is ongoing information from our environment simultaneously presented to us as we move through our daily routines and activities. Information is not presented in isolation or sequentially as we interact with our environment. Seeing, smelling, touching, tasting, and hearing all that our environment has to offer is complex in presentation, organization, and integration. We would invite you to take a moment and consider the various stimuli you have processed today or even at this moment. What do you notice? You are reading this book. Are there sounds around you? Are you currently eating a snack or drinking water? Are you holding the book while reading? Consider all the sensory information you are experiencing just in this one single moment in time. It is likely becoming very clear that you do not process one piece of information at a time, but instead are receiving, processing, organizing, and integrating familiar and novel information throughout your day. You might also notice that you aren't asked if you are ready to receive all the information presented to you or how you would like it presented. The information is received whether we are ready or not, which can impact our ability to process. Feeling tired, sick, or stressed can all impact how efficiently and effectively we process the information we are receiving during our daily routines and interactions.

There is no question that we have a significant amount of multisensory information to process each day. As we begin to explore the path of sound, notice all the auditory input you are receiving continuously during your day. Notice that some auditory information is in the absence of other stimuli, while other auditory stimuli are combined with visual or tactile stimuli. If someone hands you an apple while stating, "here's an apple for you to eat," you are receiving auditory, tactile, and visual information to process. If you take a bite of the apple, you have now added taste to the information received. In some cases, combined stimuli provide context and cues, while in other situations, multimodal information increases the complexity of processing the information.

Acoustic Wave to Hydrochemical Energy

The path from hearing a sound to processing is a complex one. Acoustic waves enter the auditory system and begin the journey on a path to the brain. Let's begin exploring the journey that acoustic waves take along the auditory system, moving from an acoustic wave to processed auditory information.

Auditory Amplifier

Before we begin exploring the path of sound, pause for a moment and just listen and feel the sound around you. What do you hear? Are the sounds environmental, speech, or music? Do you hear only one sound or many sounds? Do you feel the vibration of sound? If you hear music, are there words to the song? Are there competing sounds? Is there background noise? As we explore the path sound takes from entering the auditory system as an acoustic wave to reaching the processing centers of the brain, think about the sounds you hear and the path that sound waves travel as you interpret all the auditory stimuli surrounding you.

You might consider expanding this auditory amplifier to a conversation with others. Ask everyone to listen for a moment. Do you hear the same auditory information within the environment? Do people experience different amplifications of the various sounds? Do people filter sounds differently? Does someone mention a sound you didn't hear, but now that you are aware of the sound, you don't filter it out anymore? Was someone surprised by sounds they didn't hear, but others identified?

Auditory System

Figure 1.1 illustrates the component parts of the auditory system from the outer ear to the auditory cortex. As the sound wave moves through the system, the energy changes from acoustic to electrical along the eighth cranial nerve, known as the vestibulo-cochlear nerve.

The auditory system, a complex and intricate system, provides the avenue for sound to travel from the air, enter into the ear canal, and change into different types of energy, with a final stop in the brain processing center, the auditory cortex. The journey of a healthy auditory system begins with an acoustic wave from the air traveling through the ear canal to the tympanic membrane, which you may have heard referred to as the eardrum. Let's investigate the tympanic membrane at a deeper level to really understand how the sound moves through this point on the pathway to the brain. The tympanic membrane is cone-shaped, much like a megaphone speaker, and vibrates in different ways to represent the acoustic wave. The acoustic wave continues its path, reaching the three smallest bones in the body which are located in the middle ear. These bones, the malleus, incus, and stapes, vibrate resulting in acoustic energy transforming into mechanical energy. These three smallest bones are the connection from the tympanic membrane, the middle ear space, to the cochlea, the inner ear space. You might be asking:

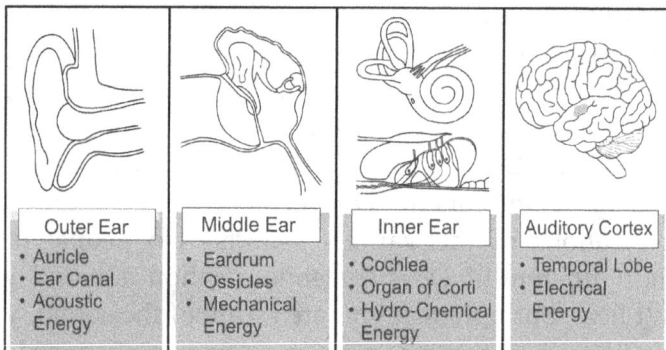

Outer Ear	Middle Ear	Inner Ear	Auditory Cortex
• Auricle • Ear Canal • Acoustic Energy	• Eardrum • Ossicles • Mechanical Energy	• Cochlea • Organ of Corti • Hydro-Chemical Energy	• Temporal Lobe • Electrical Energy

FIGURE 1.1 Auditory System Pathway: Outer Ear to the Brain. Illustrated by Elizabeth Bame.

How do these bones connect? The outermost bone is the malleus, connected to the tympanic membrane, followed by the incus, and moving to the stapes, which fits into the oval window of the cochlea; therefore, this chain of bones is responsible for moving the sound from the middle ear to the inner ear. As we continue this sound journey, we have now arrived at the cochlea, or inner ear. Remember, the sound wave is now in the form of mechanical energy as it enters the fluid-filled bony labyrinth of the cochlea.

Let's take a slight side trip on our path to explore the cochlea. The cochlea includes a fluid-filled sac, called the scala media, which runs the length of the cochlea. The scala media has 30,000–40,000 hair cells that stimulate the nerve cells, when they are pushed over. As we return to the path of sound, we find that mechanical energy is now transformed into hydrochemical energy, resulting in stimulation of cranial nerve eight (CN VIII), also known as the vestibulocochlear nerve. In some cases, people will end the path of sound at this anatomical point, but there is significance in continuing the discussion to include the processing components of the sound journey.

In fact, the path of the auditory signal does not end at the neurons of the cochlea. When traveling along the nerve pathway, important auditory information is organized, separated, and analyzed at several junctures, referred to as synapses, as the electric stimuli travel to the brain. Let's think about the electrical energy like a circuit breaker that is sent to various areas of the brain to be processed. As we continue our discussion in future chapters of this book, we will explore specific auditory processing skills and their significance in effective and efficient processing of information. First, let's take a moment to explore the concept of electrical energy acting as a circuit breaker and how it results in specific responses to sounds in our environment.

Auditory Amplifier

What does this concept of electrical energy acting as a circuit breaker mean in our daily responses to sounds? Some sounds may trigger an emotional reaction, a startle response, fear, or excitement, resulting in brain activation and processing of the sound. As a result of the processing of the sound, the body reacts. Perhaps, you scream, move away, smile, or reach for something.

What sounds can you think of that result in an emotional reaction? Are there sounds that cause you to startle? Have you ever screamed in response to a sound? Are there sounds that result in you smiling?

Consider sounds you may hear in your environment. What is your response to a car horn? How do you react to a fire alarm? What about a siren? Do you have a response to hearing birds singing? What is your response when you hear wind chimes, a train horn, waves, or leaves rustling in the wind? There are so many sounds in our environment and many of them result in a reaction. It is interesting to consider how the same sound may elicit unique reactions from different people based on prior experiences.

During development and experiences of daily activities, simple sounds that are repeated, with predicted outcomes, become the solid foundation for auditory and brain development. Consider the reactions you may have to a loved one's voice, the ice cream truck coming down the street, a favorite song, or a siren. These different auditory stimuli will likely result in a different reaction and subsequent action. This sounds simple, right? As we explore the path of sound, it becomes clear, there is complexity to the processing of auditory information. In fact, in healthy auditory systems, there is an electrical signal sent to multiple parts of the brain to create a verbal, visual, motor, or musical response to meaningful sound. Thinking of the brain as a large electrical panel with the capability to turn switches on and off, that makes connections, and increases speed and efficiency with use, we can begin to understand the importance of auditory information being shared with multiple areas of the brain to organize, analyze, and interpret for daily speech, language, and literacy tasks.

If we understand the importance of repeated experiences with sound, resulting in predicted outcomes, as a foundational component of development, we can connect to the positive impact of enhanced and frequent sound stimulation during the early years for increasing the efficiency and speed of processing and responses to auditory information. Nerves in the human body are covered with myelin, a layer of insulation that thickens with increased use. This myelin sheath allows electrical signals to travel along the nerves with increased speed and efficiency. In fact, the auditory brainstem is mature by the age of two, resulting in adult-like auditory brainstem responses (ABRs) (Kraus & White-Schwoch, 2015). The more the neural pathway is stimulated, the thicker the myelin becomes, increasing the speed and efficiency of the transmission of the energy, resulting in faster and more efficient connections for quicker responses and reactions to auditory stimuli. While we know that enhanced experiences and frequent exposure to auditory experiences during early development will build stronger neural pathways, we also need to recognize that damage, underdevelopment, and low stimulation may negatively impact the efficiency and speed of the transmission of energy along the auditory pathway. Although the focus of this book is the early childhood years, specifically birth to eight years, it is also relevant to note that demyelination can occur at any point during life. Multiple sclerosis and Guillain–Barre syndrome are examples of diseases that can cause demyelination, resulting in slower neural responses because the myelin sheath is reduced and becomes weaker. Slower nerves may cause slower, less coordinated movements. So, even if there is a strong development of the auditory system during the early years, trauma and diseases across the lifespan can impact auditory processing abilities.

Early Auditory Screening

Early hearing screening is an important step in early identification and intervention. Although there is no federal mandate for newborn hearing screenings, there is federal funding available for these screenings because of the Early Hearing Detection and Intervention (EHDI) Act of 2022 (PL117-241). In reviewing the history of funding and laws specific to newborn hearing screening, there has been federal funding to support hearing screening since 2010; however, the first legislation was introduced in 2017. The legislation directs the Health Resources and Services Administration (HRSA), Centers for Disease Control and Prevention (CDC), and the National Institutes of Health (NIH) to form a cooperative oversight group focused on early identification. The American Speech-Language-Hearing Association (ASHA), the national accrediting association for audiologists and speech-language pathologists, and the American Academy of Audiology (AAA) have members on the EDHI committee to support the development and implementation of a plan for early identification and discussion of early intervention. Currently, each state determines its plan for implementation of the EHDI Act of 2022. While some states have mandates for the EDHI program, most have defined requirements in the absence of mandates.

Have you ever wondered how newborns can participate in a hearing screening? If we are thinking of *raising your hand when you hear the beep* hearing screening or assessment, we can all agree that wouldn't work for a newborn. So, what does a hearing screening with a newborn during their first few days of life look like? The hearing screening typically occurs during the first few days of a baby's life, often before discharge from the medical facility after birth. It is important to note this screening is not painful to the infant and provides important early information about hearing. The screening is conducted by placing soft earphones on the infant's ears to deliver clicks or tones into the baby's ears for automated auditory brainstem response (ABR) or inserting earbuds in the outer ear canal for otoacoustic emissions (OAE). It is more common for newborns to be screened using OAE, when compared to the use of ABR. Let's investigate the OAE and ABR to build context for understanding this assessment measure. The OAE screening measures the hair cells in the cochlea, while ABR indicates the vestibulocochlear nerve and brain response to sound. If there is an issue in the outer or middle ear, for example, fluid, this will impact both the ABR and OAE testing. Outer and middle ear issues are often medically treatable, but not always. After the outer and middle ear issues are resolved, ABR and OAE testing will be repeated. We know the myelin sheath that transmits the energy to the brain develops thickness through auditory experiences. Since newborns have not experienced a significant number of auditory opportunities, their myelin sheath has not yet developed increased thickness. This results in different normative data for newborns when compared to young children. The expected speed of the neural auditory response will be slower for newborns because the sound signal will take longer to reach the different synapses of the nerve when traveling from the cochlea to the brain. As healthy auditory development takes place with auditory exposure and experiences during the early years of development, the myelin thickens, increasing the speed of the transmission along the neural pathway.

Early Auditory Development

The early childhood years serve an important role in the development of speech and language skills. The development of these important communication skills relies on the maturation of the auditory system (Thompson et al., 2021). As we begin to explore auditory development in infants, toddlers, and young children in our lives, it is helpful to note that auditory fibers travel along different pathways to reach the brain. Most neural fibers from the right ear travel to the left hemisphere of the brain, where the speech and language centers of the brain are typically located. Two parts of the brain that control speech and language, Broca's area, located in the left frontal lobe, and Wernicke's area, located in the left temporal lobe, are important to this discussion. Broca's area is important to the production of speech and motor speech control, but it should also be noted that this area has been found to play a role in language comprehension. Wernicke's area is important to the comprehension of language, including speech sounds. The auditory processing center of the brain is found in the left hemisphere, temporal lobe of the brain. The auditory processing, speech, and language centers of the brain are close together, providing an important connection for efficiency. This is interesting to think about when we consider the significant connection between auditory processing, speech, language, and literacy.

Figure 1.2 illustrates the integration of the auditory and speech processing systems. In order to respond to an auditory question, for example, "What is your name?," the acoustic signal travels from the outer through the middle and inner ear to the eighth cranial nerve arriving at the primary auditory cortex. This illustration indicates the complex integration necessary for a verbal response "My name is____." The auditory signal reaches the primary auditory cortex in the temporal lobe, then proceeds to Wernicke's area (receptive language) in the temporal lobe to interpret the words. Next, to respond to the question, the information is transferred to Broca's area (expressive language) to formulate the words for a response and then to the motor strip to coordinate the muscles to articulate the words. When we consider reading, there is also a complex coordination and integration between auditory, visual, and language areas of the brain needed for effectiveness and efficiency. A disconnection or poor connection between any of the areas of the brain needed for the coordination of these tasks will affect the efficiency and effectiveness of the responses. Neural fibers connect to other areas of the brain like an electrical panel.

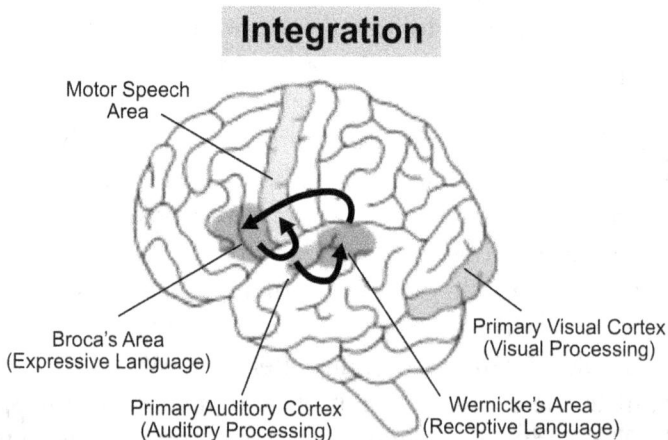

FIGURE 1.2 Integration of the Auditory and Speech Processing Centers. Illustrated by Elizabeth Bame.

Additionally, neural fibers from the left ear travel to the right hemisphere of the brain, where music is processed. These neural fibers travel across the brain via the corpus callosum, a band of neural fibers connecting the right and left hemispheres of the brain. As we consider development, two ears with developed symmetry within the auditory processing system will provide a strong foundation for greater integration and efficiency in processing complex auditory signals. The longer pathway to the speech and language center of the brain results in a typically stronger right ear for processing. The left ear continues to develop and reach symmetry with the right ear by 12 years of age. In fact, auditory responses approximate those of adults by approximately 12 years of age for children with normal hearing (Roeser & Downs, 2004). We will discuss the impact of asymmetrical processing in Chapter 4.

Figure 1.3 helps us understand the dichotic auditory pathway. Different auditory information is being given at the same time to both ears. When there is auditory information going to both ears, and the auditory pathway is different for each ear, most of the auditory information entering the right ear travels to the left hemisphere (auditory cortex) represented by the solid line with arrows. Most of the auditory information traveling through the left ear auditory system goes to the right hemisphere (auditory cortex) and then through the corpus callosum (large neural

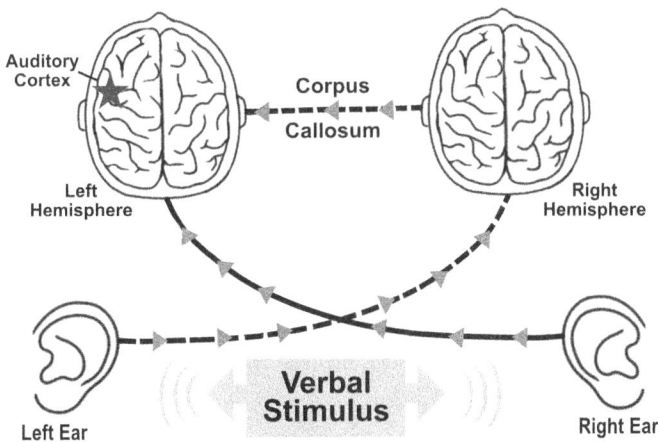

FIGURE 1.3 Dichotic Auditory Pathway. Illustrated by Elizabeth Bame.

interconnection between the hemispheres) to the left auditory cortex. The left ear pathway is longer and typically is slower to mature. Dichotic processing requires the auditory system to analyze, organize, differentiate, and suppress all the auditory information. There are times when the different information from both ears is important for processing; however, background noise in one ear and speech in the other requires the ability to ignore auditory information stimulating one ear and, at the same time, process, listen, and determine a response from the other ear. In cases of amblyaudia, hearing acuity can be equal for both ears (hearing within normal limits); however, auditory processing ability is much weaker for one ear, typically for the left ear.

We have described the typical pathways for auditory and language processing. It is important to realize that brains can be organized differently, for example, the main language center may be in the right hemisphere or connections may be different. Brains that are organized differently may require more intervention to achieve auditory and language processing similar to typically developing brains. In addition, head trauma and drug toxicity can damage connections requiring "rewiring" of the brain for efficient function.

Summary

Research provides evidence of the linear development of the brain's ability to process acoustic signals received and the maturation of high-level auditory cognition, subcortical auditory development, from three to eight years of age (Thompson et al., 2021). As infants, toddlers, and children continue to develop their auditory system, ongoing and frequent exposures and experiences with auditory stimuli will continue to strengthen and build a foundation of neural pathways for localizing, identifying, discriminating, organizing, analyzing, and processing auditory information during daily activities. With exposure to human speech and language, environmental noises, and opportunities to filter competing auditory information, stronger processing networks develop, and we can continue to identify milestones for a child's ability to process auditory stimuli. It is important to note that although we have shared the science of hearing as an introduction to this auditory journey, you will find there are multiple fun and interactive ways to build skills through play and nurturing interactions. As we end our discussion of the basic overview of the anatomy of the auditory system, we will be moving our discussion to the foundation of early development and the reliance on the integration of the auditory, speech, language, and visual systems. We hope you will join us in Chapter 2, continuing this journey of understanding the complexity of processing auditory and language information.

References

Center on the Developing Child (2007). *The science of early childhood development* (InBrief). www.developingchild.harvard.edu

Davis, H., Schlundt, D., Bonnet, K., Camarata, S., Hornsby, B., & Bess, F. H. (2021). Listening-related fatigue in children with hearing loss: Perspectives of children, parents, and school professionals. *American Journal of Audiology, 30*(4), 929–940.

Holman, J. A., Hornsby, B. W., Bess, F. H., & Naylor, G. (2021). Can listening-related fatigue influence well-being? Examining associations between hearing loss, fatigue, activity levels and well-being. *International Journal of Audiology, 60*(sup2), 47–59.

Hornsby, B. W. (2013). The effects of hearing aid use on listening effort and mental fatigue associated with sustained speech processing demands. *Ear and Hearing, 34*(5), 523–534.

Hornsby, B. W. Y., Camarata, S., Cho, S.-J., Davis, H., McGarrigle, R., & Bess, F. H. (2022). Development and evaluation of pediatric versions of the Vanderbilt fatigue scale for children with hearing loss. *Journal of Speech, Language, and Hearing Research, 65*(6), 2343–2363.

Hornsby, B. W. Y., & Kipp, A. M. (2016). Subjective ratings of fatigue and vigor in adults with hearing loss are driven by perceived hearing difficulties not degree of hearing loss. *Ear and Hearing, 37*(1), e1–e10.

Kraus, N., & White-Schwoch, T. (2015). Auditory brainstem development: More than meets the ear. *The Hearing Journal, 68*(7), 30–32.

Lindburg, M., Ead, B., Jeffe, D. B., & Lieu, J. E. (2021). Hearing loss–related issues affecting quality of life in preschool children. *Otolaryngology–Head and Neck Surgery*, *164*(6), 1322–1329.

Moore, T. M., Key, A. P., Thelen, A., & Hornsby, B. W. Y. (2017). Neural mechanisms of mental fatigue elicited by sustained auditory processing. *Neuropsychologia*, *106*, 371–382.

Roeser, R. J., & Downs, M. P. (Eds.). (2004). *Auditory disorders in school children: The law, identification, remediation*. Thieme.

Thompson, E. C., Estabrook, R., Krizman, J., Smith, S., Huang, S., White-Schwoch, T., Nicol, T., & Kraus, N. (2021). Auditory neurophysiological development in early childhood: A growth curve modeling approach. *Clinical Neurophysiology: Official Journal of the International Federation of Clinical Neurophysiology*, *132*(9), 2110–2122.

Tierney, A. L., & Nelson, C. A. 3rd. (2009). Brain development and the role of experience in the early years. *Zero to Three*, *30*(2), 9–13.

2

Early Brain Development and the Auditory System 0–8 Years

Auditory Processing for Effective Communication and Learning Experiences

Auditory processing is an important part of our daily interactions, communication, and acquisition of information. As we consider the auditory processing skills that are important to effectively and efficiently communicate and interact with the people and world around us, we need to begin exploring the hierarchical components involved. The auditory processing hierarchy includes detection, discrimination, identification, and comprehension (Erber, 1982). Given the many components of processing auditory information, it is important to note that deficits in any of these areas have the potential to negatively impact or impede effective processing of auditory information. Let's begin by breaking down each of these components of auditory processing to better understand the important contribution of each listening task. As you learn more about each listening task and identify related examples outlined in Table 2.1, make a note of when these occur with the young children with whom you communicate and interact in your life. Detection and discrimination begin

DOI: 10.4324/9781032647098-2

TABLE 2.1 Auditory Listening Tasks

Listening Task	Definition	Examples
Detection	Presence or absence of sound	• Infant's eyes widen when hearing their parent's voice • Infant turns head when their pet dog barks
Discrimination	Same or different sounds	• Young toddler picks up the firetruck, not the toy cow when you make a siren noise • Young toddler points to the toy cat, not the toy horse when you say "meow"
Identification	Sound recognition	• Toddler hears their pet dog bark in another room and says "dog" • Young child hears the home's garage door open, and infant begins crawling or walking toward the back door that leads to the garage
Comprehension	Understanding and using auditory information	• Preschooler can answer questions about a story read during story time • Preschooler can follow two- to three-step directions when participating in a movement activity at school

Source: Erber (1982).

to develop as early as birth to three months of age. Identification begins to develop at four to six months, with the identification of prosody. Infants begin to identify inflection, tone, rhythm, and loudness, referred to as the suprasegmental features of speech, during their early months of life (Hayashi et al., 2001). These skills continue to develop from basic to more refined with early, consistent, and frequent auditory and language interactions and experiences.

Auditory Detection

At a basic level, the detection of sound is where the auditory journey begins. Without the ability to detect sound, we can't begin to discuss how the sound is localized, discriminated, or comprehended. Detecting sound is the most basic level of hearing and is functional at birth. Infants as young as birth to three months demonstrate sound detection by startling to a loud noise, calming with soothing music or sounds, or becoming calm when crying in response to a familiar voice. Even the detection of sound at this early stage of development results in the observed processing of auditory information. When an infant calms to the sound of a familiar voice or music, there is required motor coordination with emotional changes. This indicates different areas of the brain are coordinating in response to a sound that is detected or heard. It is important to recognize that simply detecting sound stimuli does not result in localizing, discriminating, or comprehending. As we progress up the pyramid of auditory processing skills, we will explore each of these significant components of effective and efficient hearing and processing of auditory information.

Hearing acuity

Hearing acuity is the key connection to sound detection. Let's take a moment to focus on hearing acuity, which is a component of auditory functioning, but is not the same as auditory processing. Hearing auditory information does not guarantee the ability to process the information presented. Let's explore what it means to have normal hearing acuity. Hearing is defined by decibels (dB) and Hertz (Hz). Let's define these components of hearing to better understand how hearing is evaluated. Decibels (dB) is a measurement of sound pressure, which results in the intensity level of the sound. The perceptual component of intensity is loudness. A fun fact to mention, decibel is named after Alexander Graham Bell who invented the dB unit. Hertz measures how many times per second a sound wave repeats, resulting in the frequency of a sound. The perceptual component of frequency is pitch. High-pitch sounds are the result of sound waves repeating themselves more times per second. Alternately, low-pitch sounds are the result of sound waves repeating themselves fewer times per second. Normal hearing acuity is between −10 to 15 dB HL (hearing levels) at 250–8000 Hz for children and −10 to 25 dB HL for adults. Typical frequencies tested are the octaves between 250 Hz, a low frequency like a train or thunder, and 8000 Hz, a high frequency like a cricket or a bird chirping. Human hearing ability ranges from 20 to 20,000 Hz, but the most common frequencies tested are those most important for communication.

Hearing screenings may be the first step in determining if a comprehensive hearing assessment is needed. Screenings do not diagnose hearing loss but instead provide the knowledge that additional information should be gathered, likely with a referral to an audiologist. Audiologists are trained to conduct comprehensive hearing acuity assessments, resulting in appropriate diagnosis and intervention recommendations. It is important to realize that even mild hearing loss can result in behavior changes, difficulty processing information, and frustration. Table 2.2 provides information about hearing loss ranges and examples of sounds at each degree of hearing.

TABLE 2.2 Hearing Loss Degrees and Examples

Degree	Hearing Loss Range	Examples of Sound at Level
Normal	−10 to 15 dB HL	Normal breathing
Slight	16–25 dB HL	Rustling leaves; ticking watch
Mild	26–40 dB HL	Whisper to very soft speech (Note the soft speech sound examples in bold: sit, **th**is, **f**ish, **t**op, kite, mu**ch**, **h**ot)
Moderate	41–55 dB HL	Normal conversational speech sounds (Note examples of speech sounds in bold: **c**at, **b**ed, it, **run**, **m**at); moderate rainfall
Moderately severe	56–70 dB HL	Loud speech; group conversation; air conditioner
Severe	71–90 dB HL	Lawn mower; car honking; noisy restaurant
Profound	91+ dB HL	Concerts; sporting events; chainsaw

Source: Clark (1981).

Auditory Amplifier

Consider how hearing loss or the inability to detect sound can impact hearing and processing auditory information. We invite you to pause for a moment, close your eyes, and simply listen. Consider the following questions as you listen.

- What do you hear?
- Do you hear a variety of noises?
- Are those noises quiet or loud?
- Are there competing noises?
- Are the noises coming from the same or different directions?
- Do you think you are hearing all the sounds in the environment?
- Is it possible some sounds are being filtered and amplified by your auditory system?
- If you ask another person to listen, do they hear the same or different sounds?
- Do you both hear the sounds at the same loudness level?

As we consider all the sounds that surround us each day, imagine if sound detection was negatively impacted by hearing loss. Consider a young child who experiences ongoing ear infections, also known as otitis media. The young child experiences fluid in their ears, also referred to as effusion, with each ear infection, resulting in fluctuating hearing loss. When the ear infection is resolved the young child has hearing acuity within normal limits; however, each time the child experiences an ear infection, there is a resulting temporary slight to moderate hearing loss. This fluctuating hearing loss has the potential to result in a negative impact on auditory processing, speech, and language development during the early years (Nittrouer & Lowenstein, 2024). It is also important to consider a first or second grader who experiences fluctuating hearing loss while learning to read, developing and solidifying phonemic awareness skills, and participating in activities with multistep auditory directions. All these activities related to learning may also be complicated by participation in a classroom environment with competing auditory stimuli, including background noise.

In working with young children with this history of otitis media over the years, some have reported hearing new environmental sounds when the fluctuating middle ear fluid is resolved. Consider hearing birds chirping, crickets, or the TV with fluctuating detection of the sound. Sound detection allows us to hear the sounds in our environment. It is the most basic skill necessary for interacting with our environment, learning from experiences, and processing the auditory stimuli around us. It is important to recognize the impact that even a mild fluctuating hearing loss, due to recurring ear infections, may cause.

You might be wondering what examples of soft speech sounds within the slight to mild range of hearing acuity (20 dB to 40 dB HL) are. Sounds included in the mild range include "s, f, h, th, sh, p, t, k, g, ch," compared to speech sounds in the mild to moderate range (41 dB to 55 dB HL), "a, e, i, o, u, m, n, r."

Consider the impact on the following sentences resulting from the omission of the soft speech sounds. Keep in mind that speech is still audible due to the louder speech sounds, but with a mild loss impacting the soft speech sounds, many are now inaudible.

Sentence

"Please put your shoes on the shoe rack."

Sentence with Omission of Soft Speech Sounds Due to Mild Hearing Loss.

"Les u or oe on e oe ra."

Sentence

"The fins on that fish are really thin."

Sentence with Omission of Soft Speech Sounds Due to Mild Hearing Loss.

"e in on a i are really in."

In many cases, we will simply ask a child if they "heard" what was said. The child will likely answer "yes" because they did hear what was said. Do you think the child may respond differently if they are asked to repeat the sentence? Do you think if the soft speech sounds were inaudible due to a mild hearing loss, it might be difficult? Do you think a mild hearing loss may impact a child's ability to successfully follow directions, respond to questions, or obtain information, in some cases? Children with hearing loss will often estimate or guess the rest of the information needed using visual cues, context, or knowledge of the topic being discussed, resulting in varying levels of accuracy, effectiveness, and efficiency.

Sound localization

As we travel on the auditory journey, sound localization is our next stop. Sound localization allows a listener to determine where a sound is coming from in the environment. In fact, sound localization allows us to focus on where a sound is coming from and shift our attention to focus on that sound. It is also important to recognize the importance of sound localization when interacting with others and the impact of interacting safely with our environment.

What is the first thing you do when someone calls your name? Perhaps the person is in another room of your house or is calling to you from across a crowded room. If you hear a siren, do you turn to see where the sound originates? The initial response to sound stimuli is generally to determine where it is coming from and localize the sound. This sound localization allows a person to find the sound quickly and shift their primary attention to the source of the sound. It is a shift in focus, providing focused attention on the speaker or sound, not the surrounding noise. Have you ever had trouble localizing where a sound is originating? If someone is talking and it takes you a moment to localize the sound, you might miss the beginning of the message, which can result in difficulty in receiving the complete message. This can result in frustration, misinformation, or a need for clarification. This can result in challenges in environments where directions are being given, questions are being asked, or reciprocal communication exchanges are the goal. These challenges can occur in any environment, including home, school, work, the playground, or a store if there is difficulty with sound localization. As we explore the importance of sound localization, understanding how this auditory processing skill develops is important.

Developing sound localization

Early in development, the complex system of sound localization begins to develop. Sound localization, the initial ability to determine where sound is coming from begins to develop in infants as young as three months and continues to develop up to 24 months (Northern & Downs, 2002). As we consider the impact of this development and the early emerging ability, let's pause for a moment to explore the impact of sound localization on effectively interacting with our environment. We invite you to consider these questions individually or engage in a shared conversation with colleagues as you investigate this component of our exploration of the complexity of the auditory system.

Auditory Amplifier

Sound localization is important during our daily tasks, interactions, and activities. How do we use sound localization during our daily activities? When you hear a siren, do you identify which direction it is coming from? If you hear someone talking, do you localize the sound to determine who is speaking, so that you can focus on the direction where the sound is originating and focus on the auditory signal?

Consider how the ability to localize sound is important to your daily activities. We invite you to reflect on the following questions related to the importance of sound localization.

- When you think about the need to localize sound, how would the inability to localize sound in your daily interactions with people and the environment result in challenges?
- What challenges and frustrations might you experience?
- What challenges and frustrations might a communication partner you are interacting with experience in the presence of sound localization difficulties?
- How might the inability to localize sound contribute to a lack of efficiency and effectiveness when interacting with your environment, including environmental sounds and communication with others?
- Have you considered sound localization as a significant component of interacting with others and the environment around you?
- If you have learned new information about sound localization through this discussion, how would you describe sound localization and the impact of interacting in your environment and with others?

When observing young infants, it is apparent that initial sound localization begins with rudimentary, often slow and uncoordinated side-to-side movements, rather than in the more mature vertical plane localization that occurs later. Infants between four and seven months are expected to be able to locate sound with increased efficiency. Development continues with infants localizing indirect sounds below their head by 13 months.

Between 13 and 16 months, infants achieve indirect localization of sound above their head. Infants are expected to achieve the ability to localize sounds in all directions, and indirectly above their head between 16 and 21 months. Sound localization mastery is expected by 24 months (Northern & Downs, 2002). It is amazing to think that by 24 months of age, two short years of a young child's life, sound localization is mastered. It supports the importance of ensuring auditory experiences and interactions to support a strong foundation for mastering sound localization during a child's early years. Efficiently and accurately identifying the location of sound origination is more effective with two ears, symmetrical hearing acuity for both ears, and neural communication connected to the motor planning centers of the brain, allowing appropriate coordinated head movement to the sound source (Northern & Downs, 2002). Information about timing, intensity, frequency, and symmetrical hearing ability is necessary for the effective localization of sound.

As we consider the impact of sound localization on hearing ability, it is significant to emphasize that the best sound localization is achieved with symmetrical hearing ability. In cases of unilateral hearing loss, there is a decrease in the sound localization ability because all sounds appear to originate from the direction of the ear with better hearing ability. The connection between the ear and the brain is complex, processing a variety of sound frequencies and timing differences to determine where a sound is located. To effectively and efficiently determine where a sound originates requires symmetrical hearing acuity and analyzing abilities. Consider an individual who has normal hearing ability in the right ear, but a deficit in the left ear. In this case, all sound stimuli will appear to be from the right side, decreasing the efficiency and effectiveness of sound localization.

Sound localization activities

Now that we have explored sound localization and have identified the importance of developing this skill during the early months of early childhood development, you might be wondering about activities that can be used in your interactions with infants and young children, focusing on sound localization. Sometimes these activities offer basic informal insight into hearing symmetry and sound localization. You can use toys or introduce interesting sounds located next to, behind, above, and below the child, ensuring there are no visual cues. You might stand behind the child and ring a bell, then ring the bell on the right and then left side. When interacting with infants, use their favorite noise-making toys or other sounds that will interest your child and place the noise-making objects behind a couch, in a closet, or in another room. Playing this interactive game supports the infant in hearing a sound and processing the auditory information to localize where the sound originates. You might see an infant look in the direction of the sound or if the infant or toddler crawls or walks, they may move in the direction of the sound. Observing the child's response across various opportunities will begin to provide insight into the ability to localize the origin of a sound. If the child is consistently looking to one side regardless of the sound origination location or if an older child looks around for a longer time to find the person speaking when a question is asked, it may be important to discuss this with your child's physician. To gain specific hearing acuity information, a comprehensive hearing evaluation, completed by an audiologist, may be recommended. It is important to note that each child has individual strengths and needs. If you have concerns about your child's development, it can be helpful to share them with your child's physician to determine if additional information would be beneficial.

As children mature, moving into the preschool years, introducing games that involve finding a sound will support continued sound localization development, continuing to strengthen the neural pathways. There are fun ways to incorporate these experiences into games with children. We will offer a few ideas, but we encourage you to be creative, identify activities connected to the child's individual interests, and don't forget to have fun! The nurturing and responsive connections built during these activities are important to a young child's early development.

◆ Ask the children to close their eyes and introduce various sounds, such as ringing a bell, stomping a foot, or dropping a book in various places in the room. Ask the child to identify where the sound is coming from by pointing in the appropriate direction. During the activity, you can observe each child's ability to find the sound. Remember that you will want to avoid using any visual cues. Be cautious because this can be more difficult than we think. You will want to avoid pointing, looking in a specific direction, or using body language that can offer clues.

◆ Sit and listen game! Using a remote control or additional people, sit in a room and take turns listening for sounds. The goal is for the child to hear a sound, such as the doorbell, phone ringing, radio, TV, or music, and then find the location of the origin of the sound.

◆ We know that children learn through play experiences and interactions. Playing outdoors is a wonderful opportunity for children to enjoy nature, experience new sounds, and engage in sensory and gross motor activities. Listening for sounds is a fun outdoor activity that we may not think of when we are running around and getting our wiggles out. A simple game of *What do you hear? Where is it?* can offer an opportunity to experience and interact with sounds in a new context. Depending on the outdoor environment, the sounds will likely vary to include children playing and laughing, car horns, dogs barking, airplanes, traffic noise, birds tweeting, train horns, or cows mooing. Regardless of the sounds in the environment, the outdoors provides a rich opportunity for auditory and language experiences. Have you ever played *I Spy* with a young child? Consider shifting this fun game that children enjoy to a listening version of *I Hear* and *Where is it*? While interacting with the outdoor environmental sounds, take time to notice the child's response. Do they look toward the sound that was heard?

◆ This next idea is another favorite. Preschoolers are big fans of Hide and Seek, which involves the person hiding to stay quiet, with the hopes of not being found. You may have guessed that we would like to shift this game to another listening version. Take turns finding a safe place to hide and the person hiding makes a sound which gives the seeker a clue where the person hiding can be found. The processing of sound localization when a sound is produced from an unknown location supports the strengthening of sound localization skills. In some cases, if a child is having difficulty localizing the sound, you may see the child open their eyes during the game to gain a visual clue to where the sound originates. We recognize that young children may open their eyes when learning a new game because they are attempting to determine how the game works, but if this continues once the child appears to understand the game, it may be good to observe if this occurs during other activities involving sound localization. Children who have trouble with this activity may also put their head down or refuse to play. It is important to note that sometimes these responses to the difficulty of the activity can be misperceived as behavior issues. Recognizing that behavior is a form of communication allows us to understand why a child may refuse, avoid, or give up when the activity is challenging. It can also be helpful to note when there is a difference in participation if the child is tired or has been engaged in a significant number of auditory tasks during the day. There are times when the signs of frustration are subtle, but noting a child's behavior changes, regardless of how big or small, can be important in identifying areas of difficulty. These observations can also provide insight to what scaffolds or supports may result in increased participation because the child is more successful.

♦ With a focus on continuing to explore fun and creative ways to interact with the sense of hearing, consider incorporating a key finder with four to six fobs. Hide the fobs in various places in a room and then have two children work together to "find" them using their ears. Remember, children will vary in their ability to efficiently and effectively locate the sounds. If a child finds the task challenging, consider exploring the addition of visual information. For example, "find something red." If the addition of visual information increases the speed and success of participation, consider if auditory information in the absence of other cues is a factor. This game can be fun across multiple environments, including school and home.

Learning and sound localization

A significant component of a child's learning process includes opportunities for social interaction and experiences within the environment. Classroom environments and other early learning environments provide a multitude of opportunities for inter-action and learning through play. Children learn through these interactions with peers and educators.

Consider how a comment made, or question raised, might encourage new ideas or alternate ways to express similar concepts. Additionally, clarifications can result from responses to questions and discussions aligned to a specific topic. While the classroom and other early learning environments provide the foundation for structured and planned learning opportun-ities, additional opportunities reside in teachable moments. These moments are often unplanned, are connected to contextual information in the environment or situation and occur without expectation. Although often unexpected and unplanned, these teachable moments can be a springboard for new learning. If a young child, who is learning language, including academic information across many subject areas, is not effectively local-izing sound, resulting in the inability to shift their attention for optimal sound localization, it is important to recognize that there may be resulting gaps in their learning.

Sound Discrimination

As we continue the auditory journey, we will explore the next skill in the hearing hierarchy, sound discrimination. To effect-ively process sound stimuli, sound discrimination allows us to differentiate between sounds. Consider the distinction between the /p/ in "pat" and /k/ in "cat". Without the ability to discriminate between the voiceless bilabial speech sound, meaning the speech sound is made with the lips only and there is no vibration of the vocal folds, and the voiceless velar speech sound, meaning the speech sound is made with the tongue lifted in the back of the mouth and there is no vibration of the vocal folds, it would not be possible to distinguish between these two words. Imagine the confusion of similar words without the ability to discriminate between these sound differences. It is important to note that the loudness and frequency of sounds provide important cues for effective discrimination. In this example, both /p/ and /k/ are softer speech sounds but differ in intensity and frequency because of the way they are formed in the vocal tract.

The ability to discriminate sound impacts more than individual speech sound, or phoneme, discrimination. A person who has normal hearing acuity can efficiently discriminate both speech and environmental sounds, regardless of sound frequency and loudness. For example, a fire alarm and a kitten purring are sounds with significantly different frequencies and loudness levels. With normal hearing acuity, it is easy to discriminate between these two different sounds. We could immediately identify the safety alert of a fire alarm compared to the calming purr of a kitten. These two sounds are very different and result in significantly different responses. The prior examples encompass environmental sounds, but the same premise can be applied to speech sounds.

Sound discrimination activities

As we move along the steps of the hierarchy, we can include sound discrimination games in our developmental play with young children. The following activities and games are fun ways to elicit practice in sound discrimination. We encourage you to identify ways that you are already practicing sound discrimination with children. Sound discrimination is a great place to pull out all the same and different games. Depending on the nature of the game and the expected response, it can be important to ensure that a child understands the language concepts of the same and different. Children are expected to understand the concept of the same and different during the preschool years, between 39 and 48 months of age (American Academy of Pediatrics, 2009).

◆ During a child's early years, you can begin by introducing sounds that are the same and different. You can introduce phone ringtones compared to a doorbell. Are they the same or different? Consider what your child's interests are and integrate those into fun sound play. Does your child enjoy birds, farm animals, trucks and cars, or toys that make fun noises? You can begin to play with sounds while reading books, making a car, bird, or other noises. Begin by modeling the sounds and as the child gains interest, attempting to elicit imitation of the sounds. You can then progress to pointing to a picture or object and encouraging the child to independently produce the sounds. The back-and-forth sound play promotes social interaction while continuing to strengthen the auditory system. Next, consider moving the sound play away from the book. As you hear sounds in the child's environment, do they localize to the source of the sound? Do they discriminate between the same and different sounds? The progression of these skills begins to combine localization and discrimination of sounds. Both are important components of developing a strong auditory system.

◆ Let's play with sounds and make some noise! Have fun with drums made from a plastic container and a wooden box. Children love to play the drums! Ask the child to close their eyes and listen. Begin by tapping the wooden box two times and ask, *did I drum on the same object twice* or *did I drum on two different objects?* You might drum on the plastic container and then the wooden box and ask, *were the sounds the same or different?* Once the child is engaged and having fun, you might also have them drum on the two objects following auditory directions, for example, *drum on the wooden box two times* or *drum on the plastic container one time and then the wooden box one time.* This begins to combine auditory and language comprehension components into the game.

♦ As children continue to develop sound discrimination skills during the later preschool years, you can begin to introduce speech sounds to the games. Remember the goal is not to identify the speech sound, but simply to recognize if the sounds are the same or different. You may need to begin with visual cues, allowing the child to watch your mouth when you say the speech sounds, but can cover your mouth when saying the sounds when the child is ready to increase the level of difficulty. Begin this activity with sounds that are acoustically significantly different, for example, /s/ and /b/. To increase difficulty, progress to sounds that are more similar in acoustic features, for example, /f/ and /s/. The more acoustically similar, the more challenging the auditory discrimination task will be. Consider "pin" and "pen" or "beet" and "boot" with the difference occurring with the vowel in the medial position of the words.

♦ Rhyming is another great activity to build auditory discrimination and phonological awareness skills. Phonological awareness is the skill of recognizing and manipulating spoken sounds and words. Phonological awareness is a significant skill in learning to read, write, and spell. Children in preschool, beginning as early as three to four years old, can begin to identify words that sound the same or different, and continue to develop to a level of generating rhyming words. Beginning at four to five years, children can identify that words are made up of syllables. Sound play with rhymes can be a fun way to introduce and refine this skill. Do "cat" and "tree" sound the same or different? How about "cat" and "bat"? Finish this rhyme for me, "dog" and "frog" and "log" and, now you think of one.

As we explore the development of sound discrimination, it is relevant to recognize that for most children auditory discrimination skills develop with acoustic repetition that results in the child beginning to associate and identify a specific sound with a specific activity. If a child is confusing sounds or is having difficulty identifying sounds, it is generally helpful to return to discriminating if the sounds heard are the same or different.

Identification

Once the brain recognizes when sounds are acoustically different, the next step in the hierarchy leads us to the ability to identify the individual sound. Sound discrimination helps us identify when the sounds are different and what sound it is not, but identification also results in knowing the purring is a kitten, not a fire alarm. It is important to recognize that a young child who does not hear specific sounds consistently or for sounds that are absent in the child's life, possibly due to temporary or permanent hearing loss, the child may not identify the purring as being from a kitten. Exposure to sounds is an important component of sound identification. Lack of consistent exposure may result in the inability to access information, recall, or associate the sound to the object. There is a distinct difference between recognizing sounds are different (discrimination) and naming the sound (identification). The brain categorizes each new sound and stores the sound for retrieval. Pause for a moment to think about all the sounds a person hearing in the normal range has in their memory. It is amazing to consider the quantity of sounds stored. Additionally, there are complexities to identification. Is the sound categorized as phonemic which is related to individual speech sounds in spoken words, phonetic which focuses on the production of speech sounds, or orthographic representation, related to written language? In fact, auditory detection, discrimination, and identification are all necessary prior to association with a visual, letter representation. The complexities continue with some orthographic, or visual, representations when there are multiple phonemic associations. For example, /k/ can be represented as "k" in "kite", "c" in "cat", or "ch" in "ache". As a result, we recognize that identification can be complex.

Identification activities

As we have explored with the previously discussed auditory processing skills, identification activities can be incorporated into play-based opportunities and interactions with young children during the early years. Identification activities will only provide opportunities for success if the child has progressed and mastered discriminating when sounds are the same and different. We encourage you to use the activities we outline as a starting point for building fun auditory identification activities into your daily interactions.

♦ Have a friend or family member call your child on the phone. When the phone rings, does the child identify the sound and run to the phone? If yes, identification occurred through associating the ring with the phone, and a great result is the child can now interact with the family member or friend. We can take this to a more complex level as the young child's auditory system matures. When the child begins interacting on the phone, do they identify who they are talking to without visually seeing the person? Grandma, grandpa, parents, siblings, and friends likely have different tones, pitches, and loudness levels. Is the child able to use those auditory cues to determine who they are talking to on the phone? Have you ever experienced answering the phone when a person calls from a different number than usual, so caller ID doesn't identify them for you? Has it ever taken you a moment to process who you are talking to? Discriminating the differences to identify the speaker is more complex than identifying the sound an object, such as a phone, makes. It is important to note that as we interact in a world with increased visual opportunities, it can be helpful to utilize auditory-only phone opportunities at times to remove the visual cues to practice and strengthen the auditory system.

♦ While your child is busy playing, ask a friend to ring the doorbell at your home. Does your child run to the window to see who has arrived at the door? The excitement a child expresses by jumping up and running to look and see who is there indicates the association of hearing the doorbell and identifying that specific sound means someone has arrived.

◆ Sound object association plays an important part in a child's development. One early example of this skill is a child's association of their mother to their voice. Sound object association continues to develop as the infant, toddler, and then preschooler engage and interact with their world. When playing with your child, place animals on the floor. Say the sounds for each animal, one at a time, and see if your child picks up the correct animal for each sound. For example, if you say "moo," does your child look for and pick up the cow? Continue the game with multiple animals the child is familiar with and build upon the number of animals presented. If a new animal or sound is presented and the child doesn't accurately identify the sound, it could be the result of less exposure to that animal. If you provide practice with the new animal and sound, does your child begin to accurately associate the new sound with the new animal?

◆ As you continue to build on auditory identification, incorporating question words into the auditory games increases complexity. You might begin to ask what, where, and who questions. Children begin to develop auditory comprehension of wh-questions during the preschool years. In some cases, you may need to provide the answer initially as a child learns the concepts of these question words. Continuing to increase the complexity, while providing scaffolded support, will provide the child an opportunity to learn and master new skills and associations.

  a. What animal says moo?
  b. Where is the animal that says meow?
  c. Who says neigh, neigh?

Auditory Comprehension

We have arrived at the final and most complex destination of the auditory journey, auditory comprehension. Auditory comprehension often requires the integration of the language, vision, memory, motor, and emotion centers of the brain. Let's revisit our discussion of the kitten and the fire alarm. In comprehending auditory information, your brain is simultaneously integrating several pieces of information to create a reaction to the auditory stimuli. Let's walk through the fire alarm example. A fire alarm may result in multiple different responses depending on the when, where, and how involved. Are you in school and know there is a scheduled fire drill today? Are you at work where you know there is some construction happening in the building next door? Are you staying at a hotel that is new to you? In all these scenarios, you are likely able to detect there is a sound, discriminate and identify that it is a fire alarm, and finally, comprehend the auditory information so that you respond appropriately. Perhaps you were startled by the sound and your mind started to race into motion. You quickly determine your next actions, such as alerting others, leaving the building, grabbing belongings, looking for the closest exit, and bypassing the elevator for the stairs. The same sound, when heard by a six-month-old infant will not result in the same response. While a six-month-old detects the sound and may be startled by a loud noise, their auditory and communication development is unable to discriminate, identify, and comprehend the complexity of the auditory stimuli.

Although young infants have not yet fully developed auditory maturity, the cochlea is fully developed at approximately six months gestation, resulting in hearing sounds prior to birth, including a mother's heartbeat, digestive sounds, and voices of those communicating around the mother and baby. When we explore auditory development, we know that consistent and varied opportunities for auditory stimulation, communication, and interaction provide the foundation for optimal levels of auditory processing to be achieved for academic, social, and communication success. Knowledge of the need for auditory stimulation, communication, and interaction for building a strong foundation for future development leads us to explore ways we can support developing these skills in infants, toddlers, and our youngest learners. These auditory experiences begin early during an infant's life. In fact, babies with normal hearing and processing begin to discriminate sounds at birth. A study by Mills and Melhuish (1974) states babies as young as three weeks of age can discriminate some features of their mother's voice when compared to an unfamiliar voice, as indicated by a change in sucking pressure and patterning.

As an infant continues to develop their auditory system, you will observe infants as young as one-year-old looking to localize a sound, such as a phone ringing, a dog barking, or a microwave beeping. This development is an indicator that even at a young age infants and toddlers are discriminating and associating sounds within their environment with expected outcomes well before they can identify and name the sound.

How can we support this sound exploration and development? Naming the sound, repeating a typical action associated with the sound, reading books with repetitive sounds and actions offer consistent exposures for connecting sounds to objects, securing sounds in memory for future recall, and strengthening sound discrimination for future interactions, speech, language, reading, and writing.

The early sound exploration and association of objects provide the foundation for future language learning. Auditory comprehension skills develop during the early years prior to a child speaking their first words. The early months of an infant's life provide consistent and ongoing opportunities to build word knowledge, model grammatical structure, interact with sound play, and provide reciprocal social exchanges. Infants begin to recognize environmental cues, context, and opportunities for joint attention during these early interactions. In fact, infants use these factors to continue to develop their language skills. Building a strong foundation for the continued development of auditory comprehension skills will support the ability to ask and answer questions, point to requested items, follow directions, and understand auditory and print information needed for reading, writing, and speaking.

Auditory comprehension activities

◆ Ask the child to point to or give you the requested toy. Remember if you would like this to be an auditory-only task, ensure that you don't unintentionally provide non-verbal cues, such as looking in the direction of the toy or pointing.

◆ When reading a book, ask the child to point to a picture in the book. As a child's language progresses, begin to ask questions, including yes/no, what, where, who, why, and how. Toddlers will begin to develop the ability to accurately respond to yes/no questions at 18–24 months of age (Crais et al., 2004). Children will begin to answer "who," "what," and "where" questions between three and four years of age but will often benefit from context clues to ensure the accuracy of responses. Later acquired questions include "why," "when," and "how" (Parnell et al., 1984). As development progresses, the complexity of answers and the ability to comprehend questions with increased complexity continue to develop. Let's explore an example of developmental progression. You might begin by asking "What animal says "moo"?" The child points to the cow. Perhaps an older child states "cow," identifying the animal. As we continue to progress, we might ask "Why would a farmer have a cow on a farm?" This provides an opportunity for an older child to begin to hypothesize about the reason. Opportunities for supporting young children in exploring through inquiry, formulating possible answers to novel questions, and building background knowledge to support future language and learning are present in daily activities during the early childhood years.

◆ Ask a child to follow directions, beginning with one-step simple directions and then progressing to complex multistep directions including concepts. Children develop the ability to follow simple one- to two-step directions as early as one to two years old. Development continues to include two-step directions at two to three years old. As a young child's development progresses, complexity, including embedded concepts, reduced context clues, and grammatical structure, continues to develop.

Summary

As infants and young children are navigating the world during the important birth to eight years developmental period, with additional emphasis on birth to five years, opportunities to support the development of the foundation important to future auditory processing and language learning are found within daily engagement, interactions, and activities. It is important to consider the impact of frequent exposure to developing the auditory and language systems. These early opportunities are significant in preventing deficits due to lack of exposure, identifying early risk factors or symptoms, and intervening early when needed. These important interactions offer opportunities for nurturing and responsive caregiving, social interactions, and having fun, while building important developmental skills for future language and auditory learning. Chapter 3 will explore additional opportunities and fun activities for playful and engaging ways to support the development of the auditory and language systems during the critical early childhood years.

References

American Academy of Pediatrics. (2009). *Caring for your baby and young child: Birth to age 5* (S. P. Shelov, Ed.; New and revised fifth edition). Bantam.

Clark, J. G. (1981). Uses and abuses of hearing loss classification. *ASHA*, *23*, 493–500.

Crais, E., Douglas, D. D., & Campbell, C. C. (2004). The intersection of the development of gestures and intentionality. *Journal of Speech, Language, and Hearing Research*, *47*(3), 678–694.

Erber, N. (1982). *Auditory training*. Alexander Graham Bell Association for the Deaf & Hard-of-Hearing.

Hayashi, A., Tamekawa, Y., & Kiritani, S. (2001). Developmental change in auditory preferences for speech stimuli in Japanese infants. *Journal of Speech, Language, and Hearing Research: JSLHR*, *44*(6), 1189–1200.

Mills, M., & Melhuish, E. (1974). Recognition of mother's voice in early infancy. *Nature*, *252*(5479), 123–124.

Nittrouer, S., & Lowenstein, J. H. (2024). Early otitis media puts children at risk for later auditory and language deficits. *International Journal of Pediatric Otorhinolaryngology*, *176*, 111801.

Northern, J. L., & Downs, M. P. (2002). *Hearing in children: 5th. Ed*. Lippincott Williams & Wilkins.

Parnell, M., Patterson, S., & Harding, M. (1984). Answers to wh-question: A developmental study. *Journal of Speech and Hearing Research*, *27*, 297–305.

3

Building Auditory Skills

Building the Auditory Environment

As practitioners and educators, the authors are aware of the importance of building language-rich classrooms for young children during the critical birth to eight years period, but there is a significant benefit to ensuring an aligned auditory-rich environment. Chapter 2 provided an understanding of the impact of the auditory system on language, learning, and social interactions, which leads us to the important question, how will we build an auditory-rich environment that will support language, literacy, and social learning? In beginning this important discussion, we need to remember that hearing acuity, defined as the measurement of the softest level a person responds to different pitches, sounds, and frequencies, usually 250–8000 Hz because they are the most important frequencies for speech sounds, is only one aspect to consider. Hearing acuity is a component inviting us to welcome the expertise and collaboration of our audiologists, ear, nose, and throat specialists (ENT), and pediatrician colleagues. As we begin to broaden our scope of understanding, there is a new identification of the need to develop and strengthen the auditory processing system. Let's begin to broaden our lens to the complexity of the auditory system as we explore sound awareness, sound discrimination, sound identification, auditory

DOI: 10.4324/9781032647098-3

comprehension, processing speech, integration of auditory and language information, and effective organization of language output within daily routines in the natural environment. This long, but not exhaustive list, offers a glimpse into the importance of building a strong auditory system. As we travel through this chapter together along the path of auditory processing, we will explore practical, easy-to-implement strategies and exercises to build bridges and plant seeds for strengthening a young child's auditory system.

Let's begin our discussion with an **Auditory Amplifier** to frame our exploration of our first topic, speech rate. These **Auditory Amplifier** opportunities found throughout the chapters in this book continue to allow us to pause, inquire, and identify areas of strength and opportunities for growth in our early childhood environments and practices.

Speech Rate

Auditory Amplifier

Let's begin our discussion with consideration of a few questions:

- Do you know how fast you speak?
- Have you ever counted your words per minute? Why does this matter?
- Has anyone ever asked you to slow down when you are speaking? Have you ever been asked to repeat yourself?
- Do you speak faster in certain situations compared to others?

A particularly good place to begin our discussion is with speech rate. Many of us, the authors of this book included, speak very quickly, sometimes reaching 190 words per minute.

The reality is that most adults speak at a rate of 160–180 words per minute. Comparatively, Mr. Rogers spoke at 124 words per minute (The National Center for Voice and Speech, n.d.). Consider the impact of that slower speech rate on the ability to process auditory information. Additionally, when we consider children's TV programming, some programs are formatted to present speech at 124 words per minute, while some popular cartoons are formatted for a rate of 180–190 words per minute. So, now let's consider the impact based on what we know about processing speech. We know that development indicates that a child's ability to process will increase with age, with children who are between five and seven years of age able to effectively process 128–130 words per minute and children in middle school have an increasing ability to process at a rate of 135–140 words per minute. What does this tell us? We may be presenting information in our interactions with young children at a rate that exceeds what a child in middle school would be expected to process. When we take this into consideration, it is easy to identify that children with weakened auditory processing systems may experience difficulty with daily expectations in our early childhood environments, including following directions, answering questions, and engaging in conversational exchanges with peers and adults.

We need to realize that we are asking young children to decode our verbal speech for the purpose of language comprehension. Children with strong and developed auditory processing systems are able to readily and accurately respond to auditory stimuli, including directions, questions, and requests. Young children with weak or less developed auditory processing systems may find themselves searching for visual cues in the environment to support the unclear auditory message. This often manifests as a child who appears to be confused, distracted, has delayed response time, or offers related, but inaccurate responses to questions. In many ways, children with weaker auditory processing systems may be problem-solving, developing strategies, and finding ways to compensate for the challenges experienced with processing auditory information. Although determining ways to navigate these situations is a wonderful accomplishment for young children that should not be minimized, we need to realize that this may only serve to mask the underlying auditory processing weaknesses that often surface again during the elementary school years as children learn to read, are asked to comprehend verbal information with less contextualized language, are expected to understand the hidden curriculum, and are met with a shift from primarily contextualized narrative text to the decontextualized expository text comprehension that is necessary for learning. Consider the difference between text that includes context, including concepts from the here and now and providing background knowledge. Alternately, decontextualized language, including information that is not connected to the here and now. There is often an expectation that a child will draw on prior knowledge to comprehend and learn new information. As children move into the elementary, middle, and high school years, with slower or less developed auditory processing speed, they often appear confused, distracted, or disinterested as they attempt to process quickly enough to keep up. I want to pause and consider a scenario for a moment – a child appears not engaged, off task, or confused. How might the classroom environment result in increased frustration, refusal to participate, or decreased auditory comprehension? Consider the pace of the classroom, the background noise, multistep directions with embedded concepts, and auditory messages without visuals to support comprehension. Auditory processing, which seems simple on the surface, may actually be exhausting for some children, resulting in some of the behaviors described.

Now that you have considered the impact of a speech rate that is faster than children may be able to process, you may be asking yourself, how will I slow down my speech rate and increase the focus on the auditory message I am delivering to the young children who I interact with in my daily life? We encourage you to consider the following strategies. We recognize that it is not easy to simply slow down because life is fast with so many moving parts. Remember the authors of this book openly admit to a fast speech rate, so we completely understand! It is an opportunity to at least consider a more intentional approach to speech rate when possible or in situations when we are interacting with a child who may be experiencing challenges with processing auditory or language information.

Strategies for slowing speech rate

◆ Pause when changing topics or ideas to provide an opportunity for processing prior information before beginning a new discussion topic and provide a clue there is a shift in topic or idea.

◆ Break sentences down into smaller parts.

◆ When giving multistep directions, provide visuals to supplement oral language or break down the directions into smaller amounts of information with check-ins for ensuring comprehension.

◆ Slow your speech rate and rephrase.

◆ Use nonverbal language to support verbal language, including pointing, gestures, proximity, and eye contact.

◆ Gain the listener's attention before beginning the discussion, directions, or questions.

◆ Observe body language when talking with a young child. Does the child appear confused or frustrated? Does the child only follow parts of a direction or miss important components of a message?

Speech Suprasegmentals

As we continue our discussion of the effective processing of auditory information, speech rate is, without question, an important consideration; however, the significance of additional components of speech and language in relation to auditory processing shouldn't be overlooked. In considering the rhythm or prosody of speech production, there is the recognition that we do not speak with disconnected individual speech sounds. Individual speech sounds won't provide meaning for effective communication. Instead, we combine individual speech sounds, also known as phonemes, to produce sound combinations that are influenced by intonation, stress pattern, loudness, rhythm, and pauses embedded in our connected speech. Does prosody impact auditory processing? The short answer is absolutely, but we would be remiss if we didn't provide greater depth to the discussion about speech prosody. When we produce speech, there is a rhythm that includes suprasegmental features. Have you ever attended a lecture with a monotone speaker? Have you ever experienced learning a word in a new language, while finding it challenging to determine where the stress should be placed when pronouncing it? These are examples of how the suprasegmental aspects of speech impact communication effectiveness.

Auditory Amplifier

What auditory activities do you engage in with infants birth to 12 months that you have the opportunity to interact with? What do you notice when you engage in auditory activities or play auditory games with these young infants?

It is interesting to note that infants learning speech and language will learn suprasegmental features, including pitch, loudness, stress, and intonation, before segmentals, the actual vowel and consonant sounds that comprise the words we use to communicate effectively each day. Research tells us that infants at one to four months will begin to improve their ability to track the suprasegmental features of speech information (Fernald & Kuhl, 1987). Infants at approximately five to seven months of age will detect and turn toward sound sources. Additionally, infants between the ages of birth and 12 months develop sound awareness, localization, and discrimination, developing association of the sounds they hear with the source of the sound (Perigoe & Paterson, 2019). An infant turns their head to a barking dog, a ringing phone, your fabulous performance of Twinkle, Twinkle Little Star at naptime, responding to the sounds. Knowing these auditory developmental milestones helps us understand with more clarity the importance of supporting the building of the auditory foundation beginning at birth. Whether you are a parent, caregiver, or teacher, and regardless of the environment, home or other early childhood environments, we can begin to provide intentional auditory development opportunities through developmentally appropriate activities beginning at this young age. Remember, early auditory development opportunities will support future development and learning growth. It is likely that you are already using some of the strategies suggested in this book, but perhaps you haven't considered the positive impact on the auditory development of young children. You can now begin to recognize the value of the activities and games, perhaps add in new ones, and begin to understand the intentional and positive impact of providing auditory opportunities to our youngest learners.

We can begin to identify the strengths and weaknesses of young children's auditory systems during these interactions. Infants and toddlers developing strong auditory skills will imitate inflection, pitch, stress, and tone, the prosodic features of speech. In some cases of weaker auditory system development, children may produce monotone speech or experience tone deafness, the inability to perceive pitch differences in speech and songs. It is interesting to note that sometimes these children will respond negatively to singing and songs. Keeping rhythm, such as tapping to a beat or pairing a motion in response to a sound, might be difficult when the auditory system is unable to perceive these sound and pitch differences. How does this translate as children get older and progress in their development? Jokes, sarcasm, and vocal tone involve the suprasegmental aspects of speech, including stress, intonation, and pitch variations. Without the ability to perceive these important aspects of speech, as children age, they may experience significant challenges in social situations. Let's pause for a moment to consider this impact. Consider a time when you were speaking to someone and it was clear from their tone that they were angry, sad, or excited. Have you ever considered how the tone of their speech gives you clues about their emotional state, potentially impacting your response during the interaction? Imagine not perceiving these clues and how the interaction could result in communication breakdowns, including confusion, frustration, or a lack of appropriate responses. Now, consider how the inability to read these clues may negatively impact the ability to process the supraseg-mental aspects of language. So, the question surfaces, what strat-egies and activities support the development of perception of suprasegmental features of speech?

Speech suprasegmental strategies

♦ Sing songs with motions associated. Many of you are already enjoying games and songs, including favorites such as Peek-a-Boo (complete with baby giggles), Pat-a-Cake with a young infant who anticipates the "roll it, pat it" with joy-filled eyes, and other favorite nursery rhymes that introduce the rhythm of language through these interactive games. While these games are fun and build social skills and connection through playful interactions, we also identify the value of hearing sounds, providing auditory and visual input through the connection of the sounds to motions, and beginning to introduce the prosody, intonation, and stress of language within the context of the natural environment and daily routines.

♦ Sound games with infants can be engaging and fun for everyone, but did you know that there are audi-tory, speech, and language benefits to these simple and fun interactions? When an infant makes a sound and we imitate the sound back, we also provide the infant visual cues of the connection between the sound source, our mouth, and the sound. The infant is able to see the movement of our mouth and might even repeat the same sound or variation of the sound back. This is how we continue to strengthen the initial understanding of reciprocal interaction, the back and forth of communica-tion with communication partners. We can initiate sound games by making silly sounds and faces, constructed of single sounds, but also simple syllables, and words. The auditory and visual input is relevant and as important as the output. A smile, a reinforcing and positive response using child-directed speech (CDS), to draw an infant's attention to you, and acknowledgment that the infant vocalized, provides feedback to the infant, encouraging frequent vocal play, which is a precursor to speech and meaningful communication.

◆ The connection between music, language, and auditory processing is a powerful relationship to highlight. All sound coming into the ear has three basic components: pitch, timing, and timbre. When we consider that speech and music both present auditory information to the ear, it is evident that they share these three components. Understanding this connection aligns with the impact of engaging in rhythm games with toddlers, preschoolers, and kindergarteners. In considering the brain's response to noise, consider the level of noise in a classroom setting. Pause and listen in quiet within your classroom or home for a moment. Perhaps you identify the buzzing of the lights, noise from the hallway of individuals passing by a lawn mower outside the window, or a bird chirping in a tree outside your home's kitchen window. Research provides evidence of the impact of music training exercises on the auditory system to support the development of the auditory system (Kraus & Chandrasekaran, 2010). In fact, Tierney and Kraus (2013) suggest that music training may support reading skills. As we review the research supporting music training, pausing to consider ways we can incorporate music and rhythm games and activities is relevant. Consider activities such as musical chairs, dancing to a song and freezing when the music stops, identifying the instrument, and pretending to be a named animal and dancing until the music stops.

Auditory Memory

Auditory memory, the ability to recall auditory information in our short-term and long-term memory, is important for language understanding and expression. Additionally, auditory memory skills are important for reading, writing, spelling, and math skills. Recalling auditory information may seem simple on the surface, but the complexity of auditory memory includes attention, the act of listening, processing of the stimuli, storing of the auditory information processed, and the recall of the information. Let's pause for a moment and consider all the auditory information children and adults are expected to process on a daily basis. We follow multistep directions, answer questions, recall the words to a favorite song, or retell an auditory story in the appropriate sequence. When we consider the amount of auditory information, we receive daily, it allows us an opportunity to understand the significant role auditory memory plays in our daily routines and interactions.

Auditory Amplifier

Let's exercise our auditory memory muscles! As early childhood educators, parents, and caregivers, we all enjoy a fun game, right? Let's call this game, *I'm going to the store.* Each person will start with "I'm going to the store and I'm going to buy _____." Each person will state the phrase and insert the item they will buy. As the game progresses, each person will state their item and remember all the items stated before their turn. As adults, we should be able to recall five to nine items (Rubenstein & Rakic, 2013) in our short-term memory. How many did you remember? Keep in mind that several factors can affect our auditory memory on any given day, including fatigue, stress, or outside distractions, to name a few, so don't worry if you were unable to remember nine items!

As we discuss auditory memory, we need to consider the positive impact that visuals may offer when considering auditory input. Take a moment to note all the visuals that you notice or utilize in the early childhood environment: areas of the room identified with pictures, toy shelves indicating where items are located, children's names with accompanying pictures for arrival and departure, books with pictures, visual schedules indicating the daily activities and routines, a picture indicating the location of the bathroom, perhaps a stop sign on a door to communicate that children should only exit the classroom with an adult, and various other opportunities to connect a visual to auditory memory of expectations, classroom rules, and daily routines.

Visuals are often a very beneficial tool in offering support for auditory memory. This is particularly relevant as children are learning language within their natural environments, but adults also often use visuals to support their auditory memory. Consider the visuals you use during your daily routines to support recalling information. Do you use a calendar to remember your schedule? Do you use a recipe to make a meal? Do you make a grocery list to recall all the items you need to purchase at the store? The reality is that most of us utilize visuals to support our recall of information. We can begin to support children in learning and using visuals as a tool for the recall of information, specifically auditory information during the early childhood years. As early childhood professionals, parents, and caregivers, we support the learning of young children, oftentimes planting seeds for a strong foundation necessary for future learning, social interactions, and higher-level organization and processing of information. The following strategies offer ideas for developing a foundation and supporting children in identifying beneficial strategies that can be used as they continue to grow and learn.

Auditory memory strategies

♦ Create a visual chart for routines, activities, or schedules. Consider activities that we often identify as simple, such as getting ready for school in the morning. This sounds simple enough, right? Let's pause for a moment and consider the many steps that getting ready for school may involve. Getting dressed, putting pajamas in the hamper, brushing teeth, eating breakfast, putting on a coat, and remembering to take a backpack may all be part of the process of getting out the door for school in the morning. It is difficult to deny that there is a significant amount of information in this process. Have you ever asked a child to go get dressed for school? They skip off to their room and ten minutes go by, and you pop your head into the child's room to find them sitting on the floor playing with building blocks or kits with their pants and one sock on and the rest of the clothes lying next to the child on the floor. You provide an additional reminder to put on their socks and shirt and brush their teeth. You come back in five minutes to find the child with their shirt on, but still missing a sock and their teeth haven't been brushed. You ask the child what they were supposed to do, and the child responds, "put on my shirt." We give a significant number of directions using auditory information. If we create a visual chart for activities with multiple steps, we offer a supplement to the auditory information. The benefits include a way to build auditory memory but also increase the child's independence in identifying and implementing the steps of the task. During the initial teaching of the use of visual schedules, the child may not independently utilize the visuals, so we might hand the child each picture one at a time, but we can build independence through practice. Consider creating a picture of each clothing item and make a chart that indicates each item. Use Velcro to attach the pictures to the chart and have another column that indicates *all done.* As the child continues to develop independence in using the visuals as a cue for completing multiple-step tasks, they will begin to follow the steps, moving each completed step to the *all done* column. Eventually, they will likely store the steps for the getting dressed routine in their auditory memory and may no longer need the visuals to support the successful completion of the task. In the initial introduction of using visuals, you might consider a broad schedule located on the refrigerator, or other location that is accessible and at the child's eye level, which includes visually represented activities such as making their bed, putting clothes in a hamper, and brushing their teeth. Create a chart with matching pictures. Hand the child the picture of a nicely made bed. Once the child completes the task, they can return the picture to the chart, matching the pictures to indicate the task is complete. The visual picture representation will support the child's auditory memory of the task to be completed. As the child develops auditory memory skills, increasing the complexity of the task is relevant to continue to build the auditory system foundation. As the child continues to find success with completing one task at a time, begin to add two pictures, then three. With increased success holding the visual cue, begin to remove the holding of the physical picture and introduce the task with auditory-only presentation. The child can then complete and mark the task as completed.

◆ Let's repeat! Young children enjoy playing repeating games, so we can incorporate the fun of imitation into games that will support strengthening the auditory system. Be creative with imitation, including sequences of numbers, words (single-syllable and multisyllabic words), strings of sounds, and increasing complexity to the imitation of sentences. In order to play this game, children will need to understand the concept of imitation. Begin by modeling how imitation works by stating *I am going to say some words or numbers, or individual sounds and I want you to say them after me.* Begin with a simple imitation of one single-syllable word, then two, and so on. You may also choose to begin with single sounds or environmental sounds to build an understanding of imitation. Ensure that you scaffold the task based on the child's success. If the child is inconsistently successful with three words, revisit the repetition of two words. Monitor the child's progress, and focus on a child achieving at least 80% accuracy. Increase the connection to relevant content for the child, including vocabulary words linked to classroom activities, phone number or address, individual sounds, not letters ("b" "a" "t" is b-a-t), and spelling words for older children. We want to work toward the imitation of sentences and multiple sentences utilizing auditory-only information. Basic imitation skills begin during infancy with sound play and gestures, progressing to more complex imitation tasks during the school-age years. Remember, if we want to target the strengthening of the auditory system, we will want to ensure that visual cues are not provided. Of course, visual cues may offer scaffolding of the task to decrease the complexity for children who need additional support while learning a new task or refining their auditory skills. Imitation provides opportunities for the efficient acquisition of new knowledge through social interactions with people in the child's natural environment.

♦ We often think about imitation in the form of vocalization and verbalizing, but we can expand the fun beyond these parameters. Research suggests there is a strong connection between rhythm, preliteracy development, and auditory processing during a child's early developmental years. In fact, research indicates that beat synchronization is the integration of sensorimotor, auditory, and cognitive systems, requiring some of the same neural pathways necessary for language (Bonacina et al., 2021). Consider having fun with drumming or tapping. Begin by tapping a drum or an empty container and ask the child to imitate the rhythm and pattern. Can the child imitate the rhythm? Did they tap the same number of times? Did they recognize the rhythm? It is important to recognize that a child may need visual cues in the beginning, but we can slowly begin to remove visuals as the child develops mastery and finds success with less cues. Advance tapping and drumming to the beat of music. Music is a wonderful way to interact with a young child and develop auditory skills. Identify a song that your child enjoys and encourage tapping, clapping, or drumming along with the rhythm and beat of the music. Note if the child can maintain the beat. If the child isn't successful initially, consider assisting the child by holding their hands and helping them hear and feel the rhythm. Remember to make note of visual cues that you may be using so that you can accurately determine if the child is developing independence with this skill. The goal is often independence, but supporting the child through scaffolding is important when learning.

◆ Following directions is a big part of our daily lives, and we can make practicing and improving this skill fun! We can give directions and ask children to repeat them back to us. Ensure that you are working at an appropriate level based on the child's age and developmental level. Toddlers as young as 13–18 months may follow simple directions, such as "Give me the cup." As children continue to develop during the toddler and preschool years, we note the ability to follow simple two-step directions as early as 19–24 months, such as "Go to the closet and get your shoes" (ASHA, n.d.). We need to be cautious in determining if a young child is processing the auditory directions because in some cases, they may simply be following a routine. We should be cognizant of novel directions compared to routine tasks when considering language comprehension and processing. Consider changing routines. Put shoes in a new place, place a toothbrush in a drawer, or ask your child to get a bowl, when the normal lunch routine involves a plate. Changing these routines provides insight into the child's ability to follow novel auditory directions, not based on routines. So, you might be considering ways to create some fun and beneficial following directions games. We are going to provide a couple of examples and provide easier and more complex practice opportunities.

◆ Early introduction: Give the child two objects, for example, a red and a blue block. Ask the child to put the red block on the couch in the living room and the blue block on the table in the dining room. If the child has the expressive language skills to repeat the directions back to you, ask them to repeat before they follow the direction. Celebrate with high fives, dancing, or other motivators when directions are followed accurately. If the child has difficulty following the directions, break the directions down into simpler steps, repeat the directions, or use visuals to support auditory and language comprehension.

◆ Let's increase the level of difficulty, but don't forget to keep having fun! An example is asking a child to hop two times, clap their hands four times, then jump up and down three times. If you need to increase the complexity, remove any visual cues and ask the child to repeat the directions and then follow them in order. What happens if this is too difficult, and the child is not successful? You can break the directions into smaller parts or offer visuals, including pictures or gestures, to support auditory recall and language comprehension.

◆ Auditory recall of auditory information that has increased length and complexity offers a new challenge. So, how can we target that level of complexity when practicing auditory memory tasks? Consider how you might use relevant and meaningful information for your family or classroom environment that can be remembered for immediate or delayed recall. Vary the length and complexity of the lines, asking the child to listen and immediately repeat back the verse or line. Can we increase the challenge? Absolutely, by using delayed imitation by providing the line or verse, having a brief conversation for 30 seconds to 1 minute, and then asking the child to repeat back the auditory information from memory.

◆ In our daily interactions and communication, we are required to recall auditory information of varying lengths but also answer questions about information heard. For the *"I am thinking of" game*, you can provide a child with clues about what you are thinking of, followed by requesting repetition of auditory information heard. Building clues to culminate in guessing the person, place, animal, or thing is the goal. This activity also provides opportunities for the child to visualize what is being described. Visualizing is an important skill for developing mental pictures to support comprehension of auditory and written information for language and literacy development, including reading and writing.

TABLE 3.1 Thinking and Recalling Activity

Thinking and Recalling Activity Example: "I am thinking of"

Clue #1: I am thinking of an animal
Question: What am I thinking of?
Target response: Animal
Clue #2: This animal comes out at night
Question: What are the two clues?
Target response: Animal; Comes out at night
Clue #3: It lives in the woods
Question: What are the three clues?
Target response: Animal; Comes out at night; Lives in the woods
Clue #4: It is black and white
Question: What are the four clues?
Target response: Animal; Comes out at night; Lives in the woods; Is black
  and white
Clue #5: When it gets scared, it gives off a terrible smell
Question: What are the five clues?
Question: What am I thinking of?
Target response: Skunk

Let's explore an example of this activity that supports the recall of information, while increasing complexity and length, depending on the individual child's strengths and needs in Table 3.1. Measuring progress and monitoring the child's response to the activity will provide the information needed to scaffold the activity to work within the zone of proximal development, promoting progression toward improving and mastering the targeted skill.

Reminder: This is an auditory memory task, so even if the child is able to guess what you are thinking of without all of the clues, ask the child to repeat all the clues to you.

◆ Delayed auditory recall increases the complexity of retaining information. It requires a child to hold onto the information for a specified amount of time. Consider how this might be important within a classroom setting. We often ask children to follow multistep directions or recall details from a book read aloud during circle time. How can we practice this skill in a way that is engaging and fun for children? We like to play the clock game. We provide the child with two to three words to remember but ask the child to wait until the alarm sounds to repeat the words back. During this activity, we can teach and practice the skill of reauditorization or verbal rehearsal to support the recall of the information. Ask the child to repeat the words silently in their head while they wait. Have you ever used this strategy? Let's think about an example. Maybe you need three things at the grocery store (noodles, marinara sauce, parmesan cheese). On the way to the store, you repeat those items over and over in your head to recall them. Once at the store, you walk through the store mentally checking each item off your list as you put it in the grocery cart. Using this strategy supports remembering information when the recall isn't immediate.

◆ Here's how we like to play this game! We start with very simple and well-known phrases or words to practice the task and support the child in understanding the game. We might choose, "I–Love–You." After saying the words, set the timer for five seconds or count to five, then ask the child to repeat the words. Refrain from using task-specific phrases, such as "take–out–the–trash." There may be times a child needs a less complex phrase or task. In this case, consider selecting words that are easily categorized or associated with each other, such as foods, colors, or animals. Selecting associated words assists with mental organization and will support easier recall. As the child demonstrates increased success with delayed recall, increase the time between the presentation of the words and the request for recall. Can the child recall after 20, 30, or even 45 seconds? With increased success, consider using random, unrelated words or longer words. Recalling longer words, such as bicycle, encyclopedia, elephant, or staircase, increases the complexity of the task and challenges the auditory system to recall more verbal and auditory information. Don't forget that celebrating the ability to recall and positive feedback for effort will be important for building auditory memory, confidence, and perseverance!

◆ What if a child is experiencing difficulty with recalling auditory information? We already discussed the benefits of using visuals as a powerful tool for supporting the recall of auditory information. If a child is experiencing difficulty recalling auditory information, consider adding visuals, including nonverbal clues, such as gestures into the routine. Incorporating musical rhythm into recall activities can also support improved auditory recall. Sing the words that you want the child to remember. It is important to note that the use of combined visual memory and auditory memory is positive because we experience varied types of information in our daily lives. In some instances, you may need to start with manipulatives to support recall. You might introduce tangible items for the child to see and hold or pictures of the items. How might this look in practice? As you are stating the object, hand the tangible item to the child. Once you have stated each item and handed all items to the child, ask for the items and request the child recall each item. As the child becomes more successful at recalling the items, begin to remove the visual pictures or items to develop accuracy with the recall of auditory information in the absence of visual and tactile information.

◆ Daily activities and routines offer an abundance of opportunities to develop the auditory processing system. Consider all the ways that you receive and process auditory information throughout your daily routines and activities. The most important component of developing and improving the auditory processing system is the use of auditory skills to engage in functional and effective communication and interactions during daily routines and activities. This affords us an undeniable opportunity to incorporate auditory practice into the lives of young children on a regular and frequent basis. Activities should be fun, meaningful, functional, and interactive. Cooking, building projects, sports, blocks, building kits, and games are all avenues for building auditory memory. The exciting question is, *how can we focus on auditory learning and development in these daily routines and activities*? Let's think about a few examples: please get one cup of flour and one cup of chocolate chips, find the blue and red blocks and connect them, or dribble the basketball three times with your right hand, two times with your left hand, and then shoot a basket. We can ask the child to repeat the directions before completing the requested task, providing a functional opportunity to practice auditory memory, embedded in a fun activity. You might be thinking, what if they forget part or all of the directions? Support the child with pictures or repetitions of the directions. Perhaps you will need to break the direction down into smaller components. Remember, this skill is difficult for some children, and we are asking them to learn, develop, and practice a challenging skill. If we combine an activity they will enjoy based on their interests, we can work on this auditory skill while having fun! I think most of us can agree that we prefer to practice challenging tasks embedded within an activity we enjoy. It increases motivation to attempt difficult tasks.

◆ Building on the idea of repetition of auditory information, have you ever asked a young child to complete a task, and when they completed only part or none of the requested task, assumed that the child was demonstrating challenging behavior? Perhaps the young child might be thought to be stubborn, defiant, off-task, or not engaged? We are going to ask that we shift this thinking to consider the possibility that a child may be experiencing difficulty holding part or all of the auditory information, was distracted, or the level of the task was too challenging. Of course, children sometimes choose not to complete a task because they simply aren't interested. We think it is important to make sure that is the case before assuming the child is responding with unexpected behavior. We prefer to approach this type of challenge by asking, *why*? Why didn't the child complete some or all of the steps? Why was the child able to repeat the auditory information, but still didn't complete the steps of the task? Answering these questions can support us in understanding how auditory information is being processed by a young child and what supports may offer a positive outcome and increased success as the young child learns and develops important auditory skills during the early years that will be significant for future learning and success.

◆ We also need to take into consideration working on auditory memory tasks or "playing games" individually or with others. While interacting, learning to share, understanding how to win and lose a game, taking turns, and learning how to work together with others are all important skills that begin to develop during the early childhood years, we also need to understand that sometimes younger siblings or family members may participate in auditory memory tasks with ease. A child who is eight years old, realizing their five-year-old sibling can complete the tasks easily may quickly decide that the games aren't fun anymore. Remember that young children are very perceptive and will recognize when others easily remember. If we become frustrated when we need to repeat multiple times, the child may perceive the frustration and refrain from participating in the games in the future. When in doubt, make the activity easier until the child is successful. Embed more challenging activities within multiple easier activities to support continued motivation. Most importantly, have fun during these opportunities to interact!

Sound Discrimination

Auditory Amplifier

Sound discrimination is an interesting skill to explore because we may not recognize how often we are discriminating different sounds. For this auditory amplifier, let's take an opportunity to get some fresh air, maybe stepping outside for a moment, taking a short walk, or sitting in the park or on the playground for a few minutes. Take a moment to close your eyes, removing the visual input, and simply listen. What do you hear? Do you hear birds chirping, cars driving by a dog barking in the distance, a motorcycle or large truck driving by, or children laughing as they play? Maybe you distinguish between the quacking of a duck, the honking of a goose, and the chirping of a sparrow as you use your auditory system to discriminate different sounds. What can you identify just using your auditory system? So many sounds surround us each day and we often fail to notice how much sound discrimination supports our ability to identify and make sense of various things in our environment.

Sound discrimination strategies

♦   Are sounds the same or different? A task as simple as determining if sounds are the same or different can develop our auditory system. The use of the sounds in our environment connects children to daily functional routines and experiences. Provide opportunities for children to discriminate or differentiate between a variety of sounds, including musical instruments, bird sounds, farm animals, and household items (vacuum, blender, faucet). As children move through the early childhood years into preschool and kindergarten, we begin to incorporate discrimination of individual speech sounds and words. One way to increase the complexity of this auditory task if a child is consistently successful is to remove the visual stimuli. You can turn so the child is unable to see your face. You can also add even more complexity by using an embroidery hoop covered with fabric. This will remove visual stimuli without comprising the signal's direct path, requiring more refinement in the auditory system. If the young child is not successful when increasing the complexity of the task, repeat the auditory information with increased loudness and decreased speech rate. If the child is still unable to successfully discriminate whether the sounds are the same or different, allow the child to see your face.

◆ Matching a sound to a picture can be a fun game to practice sound discrimination. Provide a board with several pictures (horn, bell, phone) and provide the sound associated with each picture. The child can place a token on each picture when the matching sound is presented.

◆ Provide opportunities in the natural environment for the child to "listen for a minute." This activity can be used in the classroom, at home, on the playground, in the grocery store, or in any of the child's natural environments. Simply ask the child to listen with their ears and share what they hear. You can also expand upon the game by identifying the sound and then working with the child to find the sound source. Expanding on language development, once the source of the sound is found, you can begin to build descriptive words into the child's vocabulary. Building these activities into daily interactions and the child's natural environment will promote the use of the skills to positively impact the effective use of functional auditory and language skills.

◆ As a child progresses, we will want to incorporate opportunities to discriminate between acoustically similar and acoustically different speech sounds. The ability to discriminate speech sounds will impact a young child's speech sound production. The discrimination of similar and different speech sounds will also play a future role in rhyming, reading, and literacy.

Auditory and Language Organization and Output

Auditory Amplifier

Processing speech is a more complex process than many of us realize. It involves the interaction of the auditory, cognitive, and language systems (Medwetsky, 2011).

Let's consider this interaction for a moment and begin to explore how a breakdown with one or many of these systems or the interaction between these systems could impact the organization of auditory information and the ability to express cohesive, accurate, and organized language output. Have you ever heard a question incorrectly and provided an answer that wasn't relevant? What was the result? Was your communication partner confused? Did it result in a breakdown in communication and interaction? Was clarification needed? The interactions of these mechanisms to accurately receive and process auditory information to support language organization and output are evident in our daily interactions. We need to consider the impact of effective communication when there is a breakdown within and between these important components of our functional communication. Additionally, let's consider ways we can support a strong development of the foundation for future auditory organization for language output.

Organization of auditory information is important for language output, including oral expression, written expression, and spelling. Additionally, reading requires organization for the blending of sounds. It is interesting to note that as children progress in age and development, the need to repeat the sounds quietly or even silently will decrease, and the ability to create words using auditory input will become easier and faster. We can support the development of auditory organization with sound-blending activities. For this activity, ask the child to listen to the sounds and then *"pull them together"* to make a word. If we consider C-A-T, a child with good auditory organization skills will quietly repeat the sounds to themselves before responding, CAT. Children with auditory organization difficulties may also repeat the sound quietly but may respond with TAC or ACT. The child perceives each individual sound but is unable to organize the sounds in the appropriate order to identify the word. It is relevant to mention and discuss auditory dyslexia, defined as difficulty processing individual sounds of language. Auditory dyslexia may result in reading difficulties because reading requires the ability to identify, segment, and blend individual sounds within a word.

The auditory organization and language output connection can be further discussed with the consideration of the auditory and language centers of the brain. Poor connections between these brain centers can result in difficulty with pitch pattern sequencing. Audiologists assess this skill using the Pitch Pattern Sequence test. Children are asked to use words to describe the pitch of presented tones, such as high-low-high or low-low-high. In some cases, children reverse words when describing the pattern, but here is the interesting part, there are times when the child is able to hum the pattern with no difficulty. It is clear that the signal is being received in the auditory processing portion of the brain because the child is able to hum the auditory information. So, where is the breakdown in this situation? We know, based on the child's ability to hum the signal accurately, that the auditory signal is reaching the auditory processing center of the brain and is accurately interpreted, but the child is unable to translate what they heard into descriptive words. This is typical of an auditory integration deficit resulting from poor connection between the auditory and language portions of the brain. Does this child have an auditory organization issue? A child with a true auditory organization deficit will not be successful with humming the pattern in order or using words to describe the pattern. In the case of a child who is able to hum the pattern but is unable to verbalize the description of the pattern, we will begin to explore the efficiency and effectiveness of the young child's language processing.

Auditory and language organization and output strategies

◆ Children may have difficulty processing combined auditory, visual, and kinesthetic learning. We can support children in developing the strength of their auditory processing skills by providing instructions using one mode of input, decreasing the number of processing modalities requiring organization and interpretation. Organize activities to provide multiple, but separate input. First state the information (auditory), show the child (visual), and finally, provide a hands-on demonstration (kinesthetic). Refrain from including verbal information during visual and kinesthetic input. Tell, show, and demonstrate to provide the child a sequence of separate but meaningful input to support organization of information.

◆ Consider numbering steps when giving a direction with multiple steps. The use of numbers (1, 2, 3, etc.) may be easier than the use of language concepts (first, second, third, etc.), unless you have confirmed the concepts are easily and effortlessly understood by the child.

◆ We are all aware of the benefits of routines in the daily lives of young children. Honestly, the authors of this book think many of us would admit that we appreciate routines and schedules to support our daily organization. Early childhood educators and parents are often experts in understanding the benefits of routines because they allow the child to understand what to expect, increase ease of transitions, and support the development of independence. We would like to offer an additional benefit to this list. Established and followed routines are beneficial for all of the reasons we listed, and they also eliminate a child's need to organize and reorganize tasks. We can display these predictable routines visually with pictures during the preschool and early elementary years with a progression to the use of words and pictures, with an eventual transition to words only. Not only are we supporting the child in following routines, we are also supporting the learning of an organizational skill that is important in life. In many early childhood classrooms, a chart of the daily schedule empowers young children to independently share in the knowledge of the routine. Families may use a picture chart for the weekly schedule or responsibilities the child should participate in during the week. We are building independence in understanding the routine. What if we took this concept a step further? A parent asks a young child to "please get dressed for school, brush your teeth, and get your backpack." The child leaves the room to go to their bedroom to complete the requested parts of the routine. Five minutes pass and the parent goes to check on the child's progress, finding the child reading a book on the floor in their room. Let's break this auditory task down to see where the breakdown may have occurred. The first question we can ask includes, is this the daily routine? Followed by, can the child follow directions composed of three separate tasks? It's also important to recognize that there are multistep tasks embedded within the broader tasks of getting dressed, brushing your teeth, and packing a backpack for school. Even if a child is able to follow three-step directions within the context of a routine, it may be too challenging to follow all the smaller steps within each of those activities. Picture charts breaking down each task into steps may support success. When breaking the task into smaller steps using auditory input, consider using the same short, clear sentences each day until the task is successfully completed and mastered.

◆ Use of organizational charts, lists, mnemonics, outlines, and calendars are all beneficial tools. How many of us can operate without our daily calendar? How many of us depend on our phones notifying us of the next task we need to complete? Our phone calendar supports the organization of our day. Do you use a grocery list? What if you needed to remember all the items on your list in a specific order without your list? Begin to teach children how to use these tools, used by many of us on a daily basis, during the early childhood years. We can support their organization of auditory and language information by teaching them to refer to the chart until they learn and can recall the steps to tasks consistently. Visual support can then be reduced if appropriate, but it is important to consider how many of us use visuals in our daily lives. As children develop their ability to use strategies for organizing auditory information, encourage and empower them to begin to create their own organizational supports.

It is important to note that if a child is reversing or inconsistently organizing directions, we shouldn't assume laziness, stubbornness, or lack of motivation. Explore the child's ability to improve organization when visual or hands-on support improves the ability to recall information. It is also beneficial to note that children who experience visual organization issues may benefit from combined auditory, verbal, and hands-on input, instead of visual input.

◆ Let's talk about ways to organize at school because the educational environment is rich with language and learning opportunities, but organizing within the context of changing teachers, classes, and classrooms can result in inconsistent challenges for children with auditory processing deficits. Consider introducing and incorporating color-coded folders and notebooks for different classes, providing a visual cue for each individual class. Work with the child to organize the folders and assignments, and develop a plan for utilizing the system. Remember that in our world of increased technology, systems can be established using technology platforms if that is appropriate for the child. It can be helpful and is important to develop systems similar to peers, when possible, to support inclusive practices, positive self-esteem, and the development of increased confidence. It is also helpful to review and evaluate how the system works for the child periodically and assist the child in making the necessary adjustments. A child will use a system that is effective and increases efficiency, so if the child is not motivated to use the system, ask the important question of "why."

When developing and implementing an organizational system, it is important that we incorporate a demonstration of how the system works. Ask the child to explain how they will use the system and provide the opportunity for practice. It is important to refrain from comparing the child to a sibling or peer who is able to effectively organize with ease. Remember that each child has individual strengths and needs, and we want to ensure that we continue to build confidence within the activities.

◆ Do you use a planner? Perhaps your schedule is in a paper planner, your phone, on your computer, or on a calendar on your wall. Do you use a combination of these tools to keep you on schedule, to ensure you don't miss a meeting, and organize your appointments? How would your days go if you were asked to refrain from using the tools that most effectively provide you with a way to efficiently manage all the appointments, tasks, meetings, and social activities you encounter each day, week, and month? It is likely that we all have developed a system to manage our extremely busy lives. Indeed, some children effortlessly begin to use some version of a planner to organize their lives, but we also need to consider a child who finds organizing difficult. Some children require explicit teaching opportunities, broken into simple steps beginning with an explanation of the reason for a planner, how a planner works, and a discussion of the best way to set up their planner. We want to recognize that we understand the significant effort required by educators, families, and children to accomplish the goal of consistent and effective use of a planner or other tools to support organization. Encouragement and positive support during the development and initial implementation will result in more consistent use initially and increased independence developed from the beginning. Let's break down what the collaborative effort to implement the use of a planner may look like.

It is important to note this is one example of implementation and the plan should be adapted and modified based on the individual child and family's strengths and needs.

School: Consider who will be responsible for supporting the child in ensuring that tasks are written down or recorded in the planner and all needed supplies, textbooks, and materials are in the child's backpack before going home.

Home: Consider who will ensure the activities are completed and organized in the appropriate folders to be turned in and placed in the child's backpack.

Child: It is important to recognize that maximum visual, verbal, and hands-on support may be needed when initially implementing the system. It is also possible that adaptations may need to be made. As the child demonstrates increased success, scaffold the support provided to increase the child's independence. Remember, the goal is always for the child to reach the maximum level of independence possible. As the child gains new independence, recognize and name the specific progress to support building confidence and self-advocacy skills.

◆ We have discussed organization systems, but we can also utilize games to practice auditory organization. It is important to incorporate fun activities when exercising the auditory system. Consider playing games, such as following the leader, cooking activities that involve following specific directions, gardening activities, looking up verses, building with blocks, and a building project, such as a birdhouse, or a model car. You can provide written or picture cues, ask the child to put them in order, and complete the activity. The child can begin to determine if the organization makes sense. For example, if the child puts the gardening activity in the following order: put water in the pot, put the seeds in the water, put the dirt in the pot, you can ask the child if that makes sense. The child could also complete the activity and explain the steps in order, supporting the organization of the information into appropriate steps for completing the task. Description of picture cards and activities also supports the use of organized oral language output.

◆ Books are without question a wonderful activity to engage in with children. It provides a social context for interaction and discussion that is relevant, while building joint attention to a shared interest. Books also offer an avenue to build vocabulary knowledge, support a connection between stories and real-life scenarios, and offer opportunities to develop comprehension of ideas, concepts, and emotions significant for communicating and interacting. Books provide opportunities to explore organization, including the identification of a story's beginning, middle, and end. When reading a story, ask questions about what happened first, next, and at the end of a story. Begin to incorporate the concept of beginning, middle, and end. As a child progresses, the goal is for a child to retell a story including important details, but also including a well-defined beginning, middle, and end. It can also support more complex language development because books include opportunities to introduce and explain passive voice, before...then, if...then, and other complex language structures that can impact the understanding of language.

Background Noise

In our discussion of auditory and language processing, we would be remiss if we failed to consider the impact of background noise on the auditory processing and language learning children participate in during their daily activities. In fact, children who experience difficulty listening in environments with background noise may find it more difficult to interpret the meaning of language.

Auditory Amplifier

Have you ever been in a loud restaurant with a group of people at a long table? Have you experienced the moment when you had difficulty hearing everyone in the group or processing the multiple conversations happening simultaneously? We know that background noise doesn't make processing information any easier. What strategies you have used in the presence of background noise to help you process auditory information?

Background noise strategies

♦ Children with developing auditory systems may experience difficulty processing auditory information in the presence of background noise. It is important to note that not all background noise is equal. Some individuals have difficulty processing auditory information when music is playing, the TV is on, there is a projector in a classroom, another child is tapping their foot on the floor, or someone is chewing gum. These are a few examples of auditory noise that can disrupt effective auditory processing. Strategies for supporting a child in more effectively processing auditory information when background noise results in communication breakdowns. Ensure that you move to the child's level and gain their attention prior to beginning to offer the auditory information. Turn off distractions (TV, radio) and move away from other people talking (siblings, classmates, family). Find a quiet place where the child can easily see your face and talk in a calm, pleasant manner.

♦ Empowering children to advocate appropriately to support their auditory processing is an important component of the early years. Supporting the child in understanding specific environmental changes can increase ease and accuracy when processing auditory information. Children can be supported in proactively communicating the need for a space that supports optimal processing of auditory information, when possible. Begin to support the child in finding places or strategies, such as proximity to the speaker, which will increase the effectiveness and ease of processing auditory information. Identify distractions, such as heaters or air conditioners, doorways, windows, or talkative people, with the child. One aspect is supporting the child in developing an identification of the auditory input that should be listened to compared to the input that should be ignored. Visit a noisy room, such as an auditorium, classroom, church, restaurant, with the child. Specifically point out what auditory input the child should be listening to, such as the person speaking, and what should be ignored, such as the noisy dishes in the kitchen at the restaurant. It is likely that a child with a weaker auditory processing system doesn't understand that other people are able to ignore these auditory distractions.

◆ Background noise desensitization can support increased effectiveness in processing auditory information. Games played for short periods of time, generally 5–15 minutes depending on age, are generally the best way to work on desensitization. How can we put this into practice in a fun, structured game? Begin by determining something your child wants to learn more about, based on their interests. Does your child like cars, movies or TV show characters, plants, or animals? Any topic that your child is interested in is perfect! Read a short story or a few paragraphs about the topic while placing predictable noise behind the child. For example, a radio that is not on a station producing white noise/static. Start the noise out at a level that is noticeable but not frustrating. Read the story aloud with your mouth covered and remind the child to listen to only your voice and ignore the noise behind them. After, ask comprehension questions: what animal was I reading about? Always end with a question resulting in a child's success even if you have to say, "What color was the *red* ball in the story." This provides an opportunity to identify the importance of listening for understanding and the possibility of answering questions related to auditory information. As success increases, increase the loudness level or change the type of sound. Consider a variety of sounds, including static, classical music, music with words, talking, or television. Progress will take time because we are developing the auditory system, providing opportunities to learn what is important to listen to, and developing the ability to ignore distractions.

General auditory strategies

Before we conclude this chapter of strategies for supporting the development and strengthening of the auditory processing system, we want to offer a few general strategies. These strategies may be helpful in supporting development but are also strategies that we have recommended for children participating in intervention for auditory or language processing disorder.

- ♦ If a child is experiencing difficulty following multistep oral directions or directions with multiple concepts, decrease the length and complexity. Keep the oral directions short and simple. Ensure you have the child's attention prior to beginning the direction. Consider offering one step at a time and repeat. If the child benefits from visual cues to increase accuracy, consider providing pictures, or if the child is a reader, write the directions on the board in the classroom.
- ♦ Consider the benefit of working through projects together. Have the children complete the tasks independently while the teacher or parent reinforces the process, problem-solving, and organization of tasks in real time.
- ♦ Provide the opportunity for a child to sit closer to the person speaking. This could mean a spot closer to the teacher at circle time, an older student sitting at one of the classroom tables closer to the front of the room, or a young child sitting close to a caregiver reading them a story.
- ♦ Utilize concrete examples and visual representations or written representations as frequently as possible.

- ◆ Provide opportunities for peer work groups to encourage collective auditory and language learning and processing.
- ◆ Ensure that the speaker is facing the child when speaking and reading. This will provide additional visual cues to support comprehension of auditory information.

Summary

The complexity of the auditory and language systems is evident in considering the various strategies and activities for supporting strengthened skills reviewed in this chapter. This chapter is not meant to be an exhaustive list of all possible activities and strategies for developing and supporting auditory and language skill development. We hope that you will use the information provided within the context of this chapter to identify the auditory developmental milestones expected at each age, connect the impact of auditory development to language development, and consider how you might incorporate games, activities, and strategies into the child's home or education setting to support strengthening auditory skills. The important connection between auditory and language skills is significant in our discussion of future language and literacy learning, as well as social interactions. As we end this chapter, pause to consider the way you support your own auditory and language systems, including discrimination, organization, and language output within your own daily interactions. Are there activities within this chapter you are already using with young children in your life? Will you identify an activity or two you would like to try? Remember, incorporating auditory games and activities will support the development of the auditory system, planting seeds for future language, literacy, and speech learning.

References

American Speech-Language-Hearing Association. (n.d.). *ASHA's developmental milestones: Communication (hearing, speech, and language)*. Asha.org. https://www.asha.org/public/developmental-milestones/communication-milestones/

Bonacina, S., Huang, S., White-Schwoch, T., Krizman, J., Nicol, T., & Kraus, N. (2021). Rhythm, reading, and sound processing in the brain in preschool children. *NPJ Science of Learning*, *6*(1), 20.

Fernald, A., & Kuhl, P. (1987). Acoustic determinants of infant preference for motherese speech. *Infant Behavior and Development*, *10*(3), 279–293.

Kraus, N., & Chandrasekaran, B. (2010). Music training for the development of auditory skills. *Nature Reviews Neuroscience*, *11*(8), 599–605.

Medwetsky, L. (2011). Spoken language processing model: Bridging auditory and language processing to guide assessment and intervention. *Language, Speech, and Hearing Services in Schools*, *42*, 286–296.

Perigoe, C., & Paterson, M. (2019). Understanding auditory development and the child with hearing loss. In Welling, D. R., & Ukstins, C. A. *Fundamentals of audiology for the speech-language pathologist* (2nd ed.). Jones & Bartlett Learning.

Rubenstein, J., & Rakic, P. (2013). *Neural circuit development and function in the healthy and diseased brain: Comprehensive developmental neuroscience* (Vol. 3). Academic Press.

The National Center for Voice and Speech. (n.d.). *Voice qualities*. Retrieved September 14, 2024, from https://ncvs.org/

Tierney, A., & Kraus, N. (2013). Music training for the development of reading skills. *Changing Brains: Applying Brain Plasticity to Advance and Recover Human Ability*, *207*, 209–241.

4

Auditory Processing Disorders in Children

Defining Auditory Processing and Language Disorders

The American Speech-Language-Hearing Association (ASHA) has defined central auditory processing disorder (CAPD) as deficits specific to the neural processing of auditory information in the Central Auditory Nervous System (ASHA, 2005). ASHA goes on to define CAPD with additional specificity in that it isn't the result of higher order language or cognitive factors. The diagnosis of auditory processing disorders is complex due to characteristics that may be noted both in the case of auditory processing deficits and may also be identified in children with attention-deficit disorders (ADD), learning disabilities, or behavior challenges. Difficulties with auditory processing and language tasks are common to children diagnosed with central auditory processing deficits and children diagnosed with ADD (Moss & Sheiffele, 1994; Riccio et al., 1993), including difficulties with focused attention, following directions, increased distractibility, and frustration. It is important to note that the complexity of diagnosis and intervention requires collaboration among professionals across disciplines, including audiology and speech-language pathology to ensure the optimal plans for improving auditory processing skills in a way that will

DOI: 10.4324/9781032647098-4

positively impact overall effectiveness and function during daily interactions and experiences. In our work with children and families experiencing deficits in auditory processing skills, we advocate for and focus on a family-centered approach. A child- and family-centered approach, combined with evidence-based interventions directly addressing the identified area of deficit, provides an optimal opportunity for timely progress aligned to each child and family's experiences and routines at home, during professional intervention, and at school.

It is important to understand auditory processing and language processing disorders. At a basic level, auditory processing disorders impact the ability to interpret sound, while language processing disorders impact the ability to interpret language. Exploring these definitions with more depth supports understanding the differences between the disorders. It is important to note that auditory and language processing disorders may coexist with comorbidities. Auditory processing disorders impact the interpretation of sound that is not the result of hearing loss or cognitive impairment. In many cases, children diagnosed with auditory processing disorder have hearing acuity that is found to be within the normal range. Children with hearing loss will have auditory deficits due to the lack of auditory neural stimulation. Additional factors need to be considered for children with known hearing loss, including

- ◆ Reduced sound localization, especially for asymmetrical hearing loss (Grothe & Pecka, 2014; Ji et al., 2023; Moore et al., 2020);
- ◆ Reduced auditory decoding ability due to reduced acuity and partial nerve stimulation (Fitzpatrick et al., 2022; Ji et al., 2023; Lewis et al., 2015; Moore et al., 2020; Porter et al., 2013; Talarico et al., 2006; Walker et al., 2020);
- ◆ Reduced auditory discrimination for acoustic similar sounds, particularly relevant for sounds that are not audible with or without amplification (Ji et al., 2023; Moore et al., 2020);

- ◆ Reduced speech clarity, especially for sensorineural hearing loss (Ji et al., 2023; Lieu et al., 2013);
- ◆ Increased difficulty interpreting speech in background noise (Ji et al., 2023; Moore et al., 2020).

There are a few specialized auditory processing tests that can be utilized with individuals diagnosed with hearing loss. The type and degree of the hearing loss, age of onset of the loss, and aided thresholds all need to be considered as factors that can affect the assessment results.

It is important to emphasize that only an audiologist is able to make the diagnosis of APD. Individualized intervention to support the child's identified strengths and needs is important. There is not a single treatment approach that is optimal for all children diagnosed with auditory processing deficits. Speech-language pathologists assess, diagnose, and provide intervention in cases of language disorder diagnosis. Language disorders are defined as deficits in understanding and/or using language. Language disorders may involve speaking, writing, or other communication systems, impacting the sound system, grammar, vocabulary, or social communication (ASHA, 1993).

Auditory Processing

The auditory processing system is complex with the potential of single or multiple delays, deficits, or disorders impacting the efficient and effective processing of the auditory information in our environment. In fact, failing to identify the underlying deficit areas with specificity often results in a lack of progress because we aren't strengthening the area of weakness. Let's relate this to other muscles in our bodies. If you want to strengthen your biceps and do 100 sit-ups every day, you likely will notice increased core strength, but no change in bicep strength. The same is true for exercising the area of auditory processing we want to strengthen. We know that in order to progress and strengthen the overall auditory system, it is important to identify and target specific areas of weakness. We will discuss specific areas of auditory processing as we explore ways to support building a strong foundation for effective and efficient processing of auditory information. Table 4.1 provides an overview of areas of auditory processing and possible challenges that may result in cases of auditory processing deficits or disorders.

TABLE 4.1 Auditory Processing Areas and Possible Challenges

Area of Auditory Processing	Definition	Possible Challenges
Amblyaudia Dichotic dysaudia	• Unequal ability to process auditory information, resulting in a stronger right ear/ weaker left ear or stronger left ear/ weaker right ear • Difficulty processing auditory information/ low scores for both ears	• Difficulty processing in the presence of background noise • Localization • Attention • Speech comprehension • Reading • Poor verbal working memory
Decoding	• Ability to process speech quickly and accurately, even at the phonemic level • Ability to easily differentiate between speech sounds with auditory-only presentation	• Difficulty associating sounds with written letters (phonics) • Speech sound (articulation) errors • Difficulty with understanding spoken or written language information
Integration	• Ability to share information with other areas of the brain to accomplish tasks, including integrating auditory, visual, and language areas of the brain	• Difficulty with reading and spelling • Difficulty combining visual and auditory information • Difficulty with interpreting and using emotions or gestures
Auditory memory	• Ability to remember information with auditory-only presentation • No visual or kinesthetic cues present	• Difficulty recalling auditory information • Difficulty comprehending and recalling written text • Difficulty following auditory directions

(Continued)

TABLE 4.1 (Continued)

Area of Auditory Processing	Definition	Possible Challenges
Organization	• Ability to keep auditory information sequenced and organized	• Difficulty sequencing or organizing auditory information presented in the absence of visual cues
Output organization	• Ability to organize and express information in response to auditory stimuli only	• Disorganized response to questions • Provide related, but inaccurate responses to questions
Prosody	• Ability to distinguish, identify, and imitate tonal patterns, including high- and low-pitch tones	• Demonstrate a monotone speech pattern • Difficulty interpreting inflection of questions • Difficulty with interpreting humor and sarcasm
Tolerance-fading memory	• Ability to accurately discriminate speech in the presence of background noise • Ability to recall auditory information • Includes auditory figure-ground and auditory memory	• Decreased comprehension in the presence of background noise • Withdrawal from social interactions, particularly in noisy environments • Difficulty with reading comprehension

Decoding

Auditory decoding refers to the auditory processing center's ability to process speech efficiently and accurately with specificity to the single sound, also known as phonemic level. We need to recognize that many speech sounds are acoustically similar in intensity and frequency. For example, /m/ and /n/, /f/ and "th" are acoustically similar. In contrast, /s/ and /o/ are not similar in acoustic features. As we consider the acoustic similarities of phonemes, it is important to note that sounds that are similar in both frequency, perceived pitch, and intensity, perceived loudness are more challenging to process. The question surfaces, how do we begin to build a strong foundation for effective decoding as a young child develops? As a young child's auditory systems develop, consistent representation of various sounds will strengthen the accuracy of discriminating similarities and differences. The skills will continue to develop and strengthen with continued exposure and practice. A fun way to incorporate sound into a young child's life is the incorporation of drumming and rhythm. We are going to venture into the science of system integration for a moment to highlight how this activity can support development. Synchronizing beat requires the integration of sensorimotor, auditory, and cognitive systems. Interestingly, these are some of the same neural connections needed for language. Research, focused on the synchronization of beat, suggested that preschoolers who performed well on a rhythm task outscored children with inconsistent drumming synchronization on several auditory and language tasks, including phonological awareness, auditory memory, rapid naming, and musical rhythm discrimination (Bonacina et al., 2021). In considering the role these skills play in using and processing language and auditory information, this research underscores the contribution rhythm activities may offer to strengthening early literacy skill learning and acquisition during a child's early development.

It is important to recognize that decoding is a foundation skill for reading, spelling, listening, and understanding. As children begin to engage in reading and spelling tasks, we may begin to notice acoustic errors, such as when asked to spell "sat", they write "fat" because they are unable to acoustically discriminate between /s/ and /f/. Children with deficits in auditory decoding may experience decreased accuracy of sound discrimination. It is important to note that although a child with decoding deficits often has normal hearing acuity, this area of deficit mirrors a hearing loss. Often the child hears the sounds, words, or sentences, but is unable to repeat accurately. Even with repetition, the child may still experience difficulty with accuracy because the auditory system's ability to discriminate the acoustic differences results in inaccurate auditory processing. As we explore the auditory sequence in this instance, the child detects the sound but is unable to discriminate it from similar sounds.

In many ways, the brain is like a computer that analyzes auditory stimuli and chooses the sound closest to the identified category of sounds. Recall the example of sounds with similar acoustic features, including pitch and loudness. In cases of impaired sound discrimination, challenges with decoding similar sounds can result in processing auditory information. Was that word, "fin" or "thin", "pin" or "pen", "mam" or "man"? In comparison, it is easier to discriminate acoustically different words, even in the presence of auditory processing deficits. It is unlikely that confusion would result in discriminating between "cat" and "hippopotamus".

In continuing to explore the impact of decoding on effective auditory processing, we move from accuracy of decoding to the speed of processing. In cases of decreased processing speed, there may be delayed response to auditory stimuli. When we consider the speed auditory stimuli are presented in the environment around us, it is easy to understand how decreased processing speed may result in inaccurate processing of messages.

Auditory Amplifier

Consider the speed of auditory stimuli presented during your routine each day. Perhaps you are an educator and have multiple children asking, commenting, or inquiring at the same time, while a colleague opens your door to share a schedule change. Perhaps you attend meetings involving presentations, small group discussion, individual, and large group discussion. In each of these situations, auditory information is presented at varying speeds and complexity. Perhaps some information is a single word, while other information is several complex sentences to process. The speed of processing requires our ability to detect, localize, discriminate, and comprehend at a rate that results in accuracy and appropriate speed of response. When processing speed is delayed, information may be missed, clarifications are likely needed, and frustration may result with the speaker and listener.

In shifting this discussion to the impact on a young child, consider this scenario. It is the inevitable morning rush. Children need to get to school, you need to get to work, and the morning chaos ensues. Perhaps you have never experienced this, but for some readers, this is likely the reality of some mornings. On a particular morning, you are running late, the bus is expected in 15 minutes, and it appears that no one feels the urgency that you do to prepare for the day. You rapidly begin to share instructions for keeping everyone on schedule – "get your shoes, don't forget your coat, remember to grab your lunch from the fridge, and your science project is on the table." If you have experienced a similar scenario, what do you recall? Did children scatter to gather all the items mentioned?

For children with auditory processing deficits, they may appear confused, unsure of what to do, wide-eyed, and potentially overwhelmed. Often, this is misperceived as unexpected behavior or lack of attention. We don't want to dismiss these as possibilities, but we are going to ask you to consider another potential challenge. Is it possible that the child heard the message but was unable to process and respond with the rapid speed necessary in this situation? We will explore this more with several considerations as we continue our discussion.

Let's consider a few factors, including hearing acuity and the need to process rapidly. The first question you may ask is, did the child hear you? If the child has normal hearing acuity, the acoustic signal is heard. Remember, hearing sound is different from processing acoustic information. Is it possible that if you ensure you have the child's attention, provide a moment to focus, slow your speech rate, and offer one task at a time that the child could find success? It is important to pause here for a moment, because for some children with auditory processing deficits, that moment of success is significant. Children want to be successful and find efficient ways to interact and communicate. No child goes to kindergarten saying, *I don't want to learn, I don't want to learn to read, I don't want to have friends!* Unfortunately, we have heard these phrases from children in their early elementary school years, from middle school students, and from high schoolers. We have observed the frustration, defeat, and diminished motivation of children who are constantly faced with unsuccessful attempts to process the auditory stimuli in their environment. We have also listened to parents share their determination to help their child. Parents have shared through tears true appreciation when they realize their child can achieve their own success, which will look different for each unique child. In many cases, it is a combination of improved auditory processing abilities and accommodations needed to support successful interactions and communication.

As we continue to explore the areas of auditory processing, it is also important to consider what signs or symptoms may indicate weakness in a specified area. We know decoding is a significant component of reading. Children with deficits in decoding will often demonstrate difficulty when learning to read or when the complexity of reading increases. It is important to note that a child demonstrating signs or symptoms does not automatically mean they have an auditory processing deficit or disorder. An evaluation completed by an audiologist, a professional who is qualified to diagnose auditory processing disorder, would be the way to make this determination. We would note that providing auditory opportunities for all children can support their development, regardless of their current level of performance with auditory tasks.

You might be wondering what signs or symptoms may be present when a child is experiencing difficulty with decoding. Where would these challenges be recognized? What might indicate a possible root cause of decoding difficulties? These challenges often present themselves when a child is learning to read. Perhaps, the child is accurate with sight words, but when moving into decodable words begins to demonstrate decreased reading accuracy. It is possible that the child will have decreased accuracy with phonics activities that require the connection of auditory sounds to represented letters. As the child continues to progress in school, the accuracy of spelling may be impacted.

As the complexity of reading and writing progresses, moving from learning to read to reading to learn during the primary grades, increased difficulty may become apparent. It is also possible that a child may begin to display unexpected behavior responses, including frustration, refusal, and avoidance. These unexpected behaviors of avoidance, frustration, crying, or pushing the book away may escalate when asked to sound out a word. In some instances, a child may guess words that begin with the same first letter, instead of sounding out the word. We have observed a child skipping unknown words and then trying to reread the sentence with a word that could make sense in the sentence structure and meaning. Of course, there are many components to reading, spelling, and writing; however, when behaviors such as the ones described above are present, it can be useful to consider if decoding challenges are present.

In considering the second component of decoding described above, if a child can't process auditory sounds quickly enough, there may be delayed response to auditory stimuli. If you recall, in Chapter 1, we discussed how the thickening of myelin results in increased speed of the transmission of the information along the neural pathways traveling to the brain for processing. We know that myelin thickens with the use of the neural pathways during development and is impacted, both positively and negatively by the quantity, frequency, and quality of auditory experiences. We know that babies aren't born with thickened myelin and fast neural pathways for processing. This develops over time and if development is impaired, delayed, or if auditory experiences don't support the development of increased neural pathway speed, a child may experience slower processing speeds. Let's apply this to daily life, in school, at home, and during extra-curricular activities. As children mature and progress in school, there is an increase in auditory information, with decreased visual cues. The amount of information given increases. If you pause to notice, we often give directions that include three or more components, including embedded descriptive concepts. Do you ever experience difficulty with the amount of auditory information that needs to be processed? We don't ask this question to cause concern that you may have an auditory processing disorder, but instead, to highlight the amount of auditory information we all process daily. Additionally, in Chapter 3, we discussed speech rate and how sometimes the rate is too fast to process, particularly for young children who experience auditory processing deficits. When we use an appropriate speech rate and loudness level, it increases the ability to decode the entire speech message. Alternately, when the auditory information can't be processed quickly enough, we may notice avoidance of social interaction, lack of responses even when a question is asked, a look of confusion, inaccurate answers to questions, or only following part of multistep directions. Once again, it is important to note that these may be labeled as behaviors, when in fact, it is in response to the inability to process auditory information fast enough. Viewing the complexity of auditory processing through this lens helps us understand why children may begin to withdraw, act out, refuse, or avoid as they begin to recognize what is challenging or what they feel unsuccessful at, even with increased effort.

Auditory figure-ground

We don't live in a quiet world. The environments in which we live our daily lives are often filled with competing noises. Auditory figure-ground is the ability to filter out or ignore background noise, allowing us to focus on a specific auditory signal. This auditory skill strengthens with experience and maturation.

We are going to pause to revisit the path of sound discussed in Chapter 1. As you recall, the acoustic signal changes into mechanical energy when passing through the middle ear. The mechanical signal changes into hydrochemical energy in the cochlea, exiting the cochlea to travel to the brain along the vestibulocochlear nerve, for processing of the signal. The auditory nerve, electrical energy, has the capability to filter out what information does not need to be sent to the brain. When the auditory system is unable to filter the unnecessary auditory information out, all the information is sent to the brain for processing. This results in challenges with identifying what and how the auditory information is processed and utilized.

Auditory Amplifier

Are you reading this book in a quiet environment? We are going to ask you to close the book for a moment and simply listen. What do you hear? Perhaps your children are playing in another room. Maybe you hear your washer or dryer. If your windows are open, do you hear birds chirping or cars going by?

Let's consider another example of the auditory system's ability to filter background noise. If you are outside talking with a friend and cars are driving past, strong auditory figure-ground allows you to ignore the sound of the cars to focus on the speech signal of your friend talking.

It is likely that many of us can agree that listening in background noise might be more difficult than in a quiet environment at times. It can become increasingly difficult when we are tired or stressed. Consider for a moment, a young child in a classroom setting. If you have spent any time in an early childhood classroom, you are well aware of the fun, excitement, interaction, and engagement that occurs. You are also unlikely to describe the environment as very quiet. Let's consider a young child who didn't sleep well, finds it stressful to try to process the teacher's directions, peer's comments, and the light in the classroom that buzzes. When the auditory figure-ground is strong, the brain is able to identify the signal to focus on and filter out the background noise. The factors just mentioned, combined with weak auditory figure-ground, can result in a mixture of auditory stimuli that may be frustrating, exhausting, and unclear.

Imagine if all the sounds around you were equally loud and the ability to decipher what is important to listen to is unclear. How would you feel? Is it possible that a young child might exhibit unexpected behaviors or emotional responses to this level of frustration and confusion? It is important to note that it is more difficult for every person to listen in the presence of background noise, but there are varying degrees of difficulty. Are you able to listen to a lecture in an auditorium with a furnace running with minimal effort? Are you able to talk with a friend on the phone with noise from the TV in the background? It is important to remember that listening in the presence of background noise is more challenging for everyone and can be impacted by fatigue and stress, but for some individuals, ongoing auditory stimuli are received without filtering.

The authors of this book have listened as parents and children share how exhausting school is. We have heard parents share the child's frustration that their child's amount of homework is significant and ongoing because they are unable to complete work at school. We have heard children share that if the room is quiet, they can easily and effectively complete work. There have been reports of young children who behave and meet the expectations of school all day, only to enter their parent's car at school dismissal and meltdown. Parents have asked, why is my child exhibiting behaviors and significant fatigue at home when the teachers report they have great days at school? So many parents, so many children, who all experience the frustration and fatigue of an overly taxed auditory system.

Children with an auditory figure-ground deficit cannot separate signal from noise. Notice we didn't say, these children will not or that they don't want to. They are not ignoring, acting out, or exhibiting stubborn behavior. Think about this fact for a moment. All the auditory information is traveling to the brain with equal "loudness," and these children are unable to ignore the background noise and focus on the auditory signal. In fact, the first thought in many cases is that the child has ADD. The authors of this book are not trained to diagnose ADD, and we are aware that some children do have attention deficits. While some children do, in fact, have ADD, some children are actually experiencing difficulty filtering out the background noise to attend to the acoustic signal. We often ask parents to consider if the child is able to maintain focus on a visual or hands on task, such as blocks, drawing, crafts, or watching a video without being distracted. Is it possible that the difficulty attending is only related to listening, auditory, or verbal tasks, in the absence of visual or tactile activities?

The challenge that presents itself in many cases is that a child with an auditory figure-ground deficit appears to hear everything. Remember, this only indicates hearing acuity but does not indicate auditory processing. The issue resides in the inability to identify and process the important information. A key component to consider is, what happens when the background noise is eliminated? Is the child able to respond with increased efficiency and accuracy to auditory stimuli?

Consider this contextual example. A second grader is participating in a whole class activity in the classroom. The teacher offers a verbal three-step direction without visual cues. *Get a piece of lined paper from the shelf by the window, take a pencil from the shelf by the door, and write your name at the top of the page.* There is the background noise of students moving around the classroom and talking. The teacher offered directions with one repetition. Consider a child with an auditory figure-ground deficit in this situation. The child is unable to filter out the noise of moving and talking peers, and as a result, does not find success in following the directions. Let's slightly adapt this situation to support success. Would the child find increased success if the teacher gained the student's attention prior to beginning the direction by simply standing closer to the student's desk? What if the teacher asked students to please wait to begin moving until the directions had all been given? The teacher might also incorporate some visual gestures pointing to the locations of the paper and pencil and showing a piece of paper to indicate where names should be written. These simple changes have the potential to decrease the auditory processing load and support the student in finding success. We can identify the importance of success for this student when considering accuracy, but we must also consider the impact on student confidence and motivation.

Signs and symptoms indicating a possible auditory figure-ground deficit may include difficulty accurately interpreting speech when background noise is present. If the child is able to follow multistep directions without visual cues with ease in a quiet room but experiences difficulty with single-step directions in a classroom that includes the typical and expected background noise of a learning environment, it may be important to consider whether the child experiences difficulty filtering out the background noise to focus on the auditory direction. It is important to recognize that fatigue, anxiety, and stress may also impact the ability to filter background noise. Additionally, a child experiencing difficulty focusing on a task in an environment with background noise may indicate difficulty filtering. It is important to note that in many cases these children may accurately and efficiently follow directions, answer questions, and carry on a focused conversation in environments without background noise. Additional signs and symptoms that may indicate difficulty with auditory figure-ground could include a child covering their ears when an environment becomes noisy. In some cases, a child doesn't want to be in the cafeteria or gymnasium at school due to the level of loudness. A child might ask other children to be quiet or may demonstrate frustration when others are talking when they are trying to listen. In some cases, a child may ask to move to a quieter place to work on assignments or want to wear earplugs, which, if fostered appropriately, can begin to build the child's self-advocacy skills. Additionally, a child may appear to daydream or fidget during large group or whole class activities.

It is important to note that everyone has areas of strength and areas that are weaker. Weaknesses alone do not constitute the need for a referral. It is important to identify if and how the area of weakness impacts functional performance. It is possible to have areas of weakness that have a limited impact on functionality and efficiency. It is also important to consider that impact can surface in various aspects of an individual's life, including academic, work, social, and communication. Oftentimes, when we meet adolescents and young adults, we begin to quickly identify compensatory strategies they have developed to support their ability to function effectively and efficiently across various environments. On a positive note, these children, adolescents, and young adults are strong examples of persistence, creative thinking, problem-solving, and resilience. Alternately, they often report fatigue, exhaustion, frustration, or demonstrate avoidance behaviors. It is always important to remember that behavior is communication. When a behavior occurs, positive or negative, there is communication. Determining what is being communicated can be challenging but is important for identifying the root cause with a focus on strengths-based solutions.

We mentioned above that children, adolescents, and young adults have expressed the impact of difficulty with processing auditory information in the presence of background noise, but we would be remiss if we assume the challenge doesn't begin until the late elementary, middle, high school, or beyond years. Consider a young child who is learning speech and language with the rapid input of experiences, interactions, and learning opportunities present during the critical early childhood years. If a young child is exposed to rich language and literacy opportunities, supporting future reading and literacy success, but the child experiences difficulty with processing auditory information in the presence of background noise, there is the potential for the child to experience challenges with connecting meaning to the auditory information they hear within daily interactions and routines. Weaker early language foundations, including vocabulary, phonemic awareness, and auditory comprehension, may increase the risk of future reading and literacy difficulties.

There are activities that can support the development and even improve the ability to process auditory information in the presence of background noise. Desensitization to background noise is a strategy that we often use during intervention. The exciting and challenging part of early childhood environments is that they provide opportunities for practice; however, there are times when we need to adapt the background noise to meet the current ability to process. The focus should be on supporting the child in identifying the auditory information that is important to listen to and what isn't. In some situations, it can be helpful to amplify the auditory information that should be listened to and processed. One way to amplify sounds when there is an identified auditory processing deficit specific to auditory figure-ground is by using a frequency modulation (FM) system, allowing the speaker's voice to remain at an audible level above background noise even when the listener's distance from the speaker increases.

Auditory memory

We know that reading is a significant part of life in environments full of literacy opportunities. Auditory memory is a significant component of reading. Of course, infants aren't born reading, but they acquire significant language and cognitive information during the early years prior to learning to read. The development of auditory memory skills for toddlers and preschoolers prepares children for classroom expectations. The early childhood years provide learning environments with increased visual cues but progresses to primarily auditory directions and content delivery.

Auditory Amplifier

Let's pause for a moment before we dive too far into auditory memory. We are all aware that infants aren't born reading. Yet, reading is important for navigating the world around us and learning new concepts, information, and ideas. Consider how infants and young children gain information to follow directions, complete multistep tasks, and complete routines without reading.

Think about a young child in your life. Prior to learning to read or if the child is not yet reading, what did you notice? We live in a world of word clues, but how else does a child learn and remember during the early years?

You likely identified that prior to learning to read, children rely primarily on their auditory and visual memory to follow single-step and multistep directions, complete tasks, and follow daily routines. It is important to emphasize that daily tasks may seem simple in practice, but there is significant complexity in processing the information related to these activities, combined with carrying out the activities and tasks. The auditory hierarchy composed of auditory discrimination, identification, and comprehension requires varying levels of auditory memory ability. When we consider a young infant or toddler learning to identify a specific animal associated with the sound the animal makes or playing the fun game of pointing to their nose, then their eyes, and their mouth, auditory and visual memory are developing. Have you ever considered that morning routines that help us start each new day support the development of auditory and visual memory? In fact, you may begin to notice a young child already demonstrating a preference for either auditory or visual cues when asked to complete tasks or participate in routines. Alternately, some children are equally comfortable and accurate with auditory or visual information and cues.

During our interactions, it is natural to provide visual cues. We may point and express emotions through our facial expressions or body language. It is natural to look in the direction of the object we are describing. All of these visual cues offer important auditory memory clues. As a result of these natural visual cues, there are times when auditory memory difficulties are not identified as quickly. When we consider the significant amount of visual and auditory cues that are given during the early years, it becomes clear why a child may appear to suddenly experience difficulty with auditory memory as visual cues decrease. Consider the progression of cues during the school years. Early in a young child's school career, there are often visual schedules, the rhythm of songs to introduce new concepts or directions, repetition combined with gestures to support comprehension, and narrative contexts. These opportunities provide visual cues but are also important for the development of language. Children can build word associations, increase vocabulary, develop a growing understanding of how language works, including grammar and word structure. As a child moves through school and there is a shift from learning to read to reading to learn, there is often a varying level of visual cues. There is a shift from narrative contexts to increased use of expository language for learning. This shift to less contextual language, expectations for increased independence in organization, developing schedules, tracking assignments, and combined reading, writing, and speaking tasks with multiple directions, may result in decreased accuracy, increased frustration, and in some cases, what appears to be new challenges that didn't exist before.

Let's break this down further in considering this progression. We often ask questions in the same way across various contexts. It is important to realize that asking questions in the same way may not support a child's development of using auditory memory at an advanced level. Children are often attuned to context cues, routines, and patterns, allowing them to respond with accurate response without using advanced auditory recall skills. What does this look like in our daily interactions with young children? For example, if the child is presented with a question organized with the same structure and in the same order, a child may begin to develop an understanding of the pattern and routine that may mask if they are able to process auditory information across various structures. If we ask a child what sounds animals make using the same pattern: *What does a cow say?; What does a duck say?; What does a dog say?*, the child may begin to utilize the structured question to identify the animal sounds are the correct answer. If we want to identify a child's auditory ability, we need to change the question structure or change the question. For example, we could move to asking the child *which animal says moo?* Ensure that when asking the child questions, you switch the order of animals you ask. If the order is always the same, the child may identify the pattern and answer accurately using rote memory responses. If we consider how we can ensure this is an auditory-only task, without visual cues, you can cover your mouth or have the child facing away from you to practice using only auditory information to answer the questions.

Auditory Amplifier

Auditory memory is an important component of our daily lives as adults. Whether we recognize it or not, we utilize auditory memory to effectively carry out many tasks in our daily schedules, interactions, and routines. As we think about auditory memory tasks, it becomes apparent that adults develop strategies for success.

Let's consider ways that you use strategies for auditory memory success. Do you use any of the following strategies for auditory memory success?

- Writing a grocery list;
- Writing down appointments on your calendar;
- Making a "to-do" list for daily or weekly activities;
- Writing down an address or a phone number.

Do you use any of these strategies? What other strategies do you use on a regular basis?

There is an additional component that is significant to consider in this discussion. You may not need auditory memory strategies for all tasks. For simple tasks like going to the kitchen to get a friend a requested glass of water, strategies may not be needed. Pause to consider when you implement auditory memory strategies to ensure success. Do you always write down your grocery list or if it is short, are you more able to recall without visual cues? How many items can you recall from memory? Do you need to write a list for two items, five items, ten or more items? Do you need to write down all appointments, if they are happening today, next week, or in a month? It is important to note that we all use strategies and that additional factors, including fatigue and stress, can impact the effectiveness and efficiency of our auditory memory.

Young children use auditory and visual stimuli to interact, learn, and engage with their environments. Oftentimes, the auditory and visual systems are used together simultaneously to process information. We can use songs with motions, books with more pictures than text, pointing to and naming objects supporting the development of auditory and visual memory. Children benefit from the development of both of these sensory systems because they continue to be important for learning, interacting, and engaging. As children continue to develop their auditory skills, we can take opportunities to limit the visual cues at times to identify the ongoing development of auditory processing skills.

Auditory memory activities

◆ Reading is a wonderful avenue to interact and connect with young children. The opportunities to build vocabulary, listening skills, language comprehension, sound awareness, and so many other skills are plentiful. How might we begin to identify and note a child's development of auditory skills during reading? While reading favorite books, pause to allow the child the opportunity to fill in the word or point to a picture in the book. Consider encouraging the young child to clap or sing along when books include rhyming or repetition.

◆ Another fun activity for interacting and engaging a child in auditory and language learning is through singing songs. Encouraging a young child to sing along and fill in sounds and then words builds listening skills. For example, consider songs with animal sounds. Does the child listen to the song and respond at the appropriate points in the song if you pause? Does the child insert the accurate accompanying song motions for a song? These will indicate the child is listening for auditory cues during the song. You will want to observe if the child is able to independently respond or if they are looking for environmental cues or following their peers.

◆ Ask the child, without the use of visual cues, to get their shoes, a toy, or a book. Keep in mind that pointing, showing, or eye gaze can provide visual cues to the child. Are they able to independently obtain the requested item without visual cues? If they aren't successful, when you support them with a visual cue, such as pointing, are they successful? Does the child require auditory and visual cues to find success?

◆ Practice counting aloud or reciting a predictable list of words without visual cues.

◆ Support the child in learning their address, phone number, and their full name.

◆ Our lives are full of directions and routines. Build a foundation routine that is built upon a pattern. The child will learn the routine. What happens if you change the order of the routine and use only verbal directions? For example, a bedtime routine, including brush your teeth, get a drink of water, and put on your pajamas, is changed to put on your pajamas, brush your teeth, and get a drink of water. Does the child recognize the change in order? Is the child able to follow the new routine as easily or does this result in frustration? Does the child lack recognition of the new routine and proceed with the learned pattern or does the child appear confused by the change?

◆ Let's explore another scenario. You ask a child to pick up their toys, put them away on the toy shelf, and wash their hands for lunch. What happens? Does the child complete the first task or only the last task? Does the child start playing somewhere else without completing any of the requested tasks? If you walk alongside the child and provide visual cues and repeat each step individually, do they complete the tasks with ease? It is important to note that in cases of weaker or less developed auditory memory, a child is not stubborn, defiant, or lazy. Oftentimes, the child wants to be successful but needs the support to find that success. Providing visual, tactile, and verbal cues can support the child in finding success.

◆ Our environments are full of auditory directions, combined with competing background noise. When asking the child to repeat auditory directions back to you, are they able? Are the directions repeated back in order? Consider if repeating and completing one-step directions is successful, but when adding an additional step, there is a breakdown resulting in less success. In cases where additional information decreases success, consider providing only the necessary information. We often use more words than needed when giving instructions. We might say, *go brush your teeth, make sure you brush your teeth in the back of your mouth, and please don't leave the water running*. These are all important, but what is the goal? We want the child to brush their teeth, so for children who benefit from less words, we could simply state, *brush your teeth*.

◆ As you are reading books with a child, pause to ask questions about the story. Books offer the benefit of visual and context clues to support comprehension. Ask the child simple questions and then increase complexity as they develop higher level comprehension and critical thinking skills. Initially, ask the child to point to pictures. As the child's language skills progress, begin asking what, who, where, when, why, and how questions. You can then move to asking the young child questions related to predicting outcomes and using problem-solving skills.

Auditory memory strategies

♦ Let's repeat and say words together. During this game, the adult will say words and then ask the child to repeat the same words in the same order. When you begin playing this game, start with words and sequences that typically go together. For example, the number one and two; milk and cookies; or fork and spoon. Complexity can be developed by increasing the number of words, decreasing the association of the words, and covering your mouth when providing the word sequence. You can also increase complexity by pausing for one second between each word or asking the child to wait to provide the sequence back to you for 1, 3, 5, 10, 15, and eventually even 60 seconds. Multisyllabic words will also offer increased complexity (monopoly, spaghetti, oatmeal).

♦ Reauditorization is a strategy for building auditory memory. Support the child in learning to repeat words audibly, quietly, and eventually in their head while waiting to repeat the words. As adults, we might use this strategy if we are trying to remember a list of items. For example, I need to go to the utility closet and get one roll of paper towel, two bottles of soap, and one roll of toilet paper. We might repeat that on our way to the utility closet to ensure we come back with all the items we need without writing them down. Have you ever experienced a time when you were on your way to get a list of items, were stopped in the hallway to answer a question, got to the utility closet, and could only remember two of the things you needed?

◆ Using tangible items can support auditory memory. Provide the child with a tangible item that will represent an auditory direction. Place a blue block on the chair representing putting papers from their mailbox into a backpack and the red block on the table representing putting on their coat. Review with the child what each block represents and then invite the child to complete the tasks. When the child returns, support them in reviewing what the blocks represented and determine if the tasks were completed. The tangible items help the child remember that two tasks need to be completed and incorporate visual memory in combination with auditory memory.

◆ It can be fun to play an imitation game with directions. The child is given one direction, repeats it back, and then completes the task. As the child is successful, trying longer or more complex sequences, and directions including concepts can be fun. This should be a fun game, so don't be afraid to be silly, laugh, and have fun! Make sure to celebrate the child's success to encourage ongoing practice with this fun game.

◆ Use a visual chart for chores or home responsibilities. These visual supports can increase independence, support motivation, and develop opportunities for success. Children want to succeed and meet expectations. Providing the tools for success as they are learning and developing builds a foundation for future motivation.

◆ Incorporate auditory fun into daily activities, including cooking, building projects, sports, and even building blocks! You are likely already using auditory practice in these activities and interactions. It can be helpful to ask the child to repeat the directions before completing the task. It provides information so that you can fill in the gaps if there are any. Support the child in finding success through repeating, implementing tactile cues, shortening the direction, or providing visual cues. Finding activities the child already finds interesting and enjoyable supports practicing and developing auditory skills within a fun context. Learning should be fun!

♦ Cooking fun: For young children, you might ask them to get chocolate chips and butter. For older children, you might ask them to get one cup of flour and one teaspoon of salt.

♦ Building block fun: You can take turns with you providing some directions and the child providing others. You will also be incorporating language learning into this activity. You might ask a child to place two blue building pieces in a line and then connect them with a red piece on top and in the middle. If you need to simplify the task, you might ask the child to give you two blue pieces and one red piece.

♦ Sports fun: If the child enjoys movement activities, auditory opportunities can be easily incorporated. You might ask the child to dribble the basketball three times with their right hand and two times with their left hand before shooting a basket. Then the child can give you a direction to follow.

As children are developing their auditory skills, and for children who may be experiencing difficulty with one or more of the auditory processing areas, it can be helpful to consider the approach we use for developing opportunities for practice. Motivation is an important component of successful practice and skill development. We have found building on the premise of embedding practice with more difficult and complex skills within the context of success is beneficial.

1. Begin with a simple task that will result in the child finding success.
2. Incorporate more challenging, complex, and difficult auditory tasks.
3. Always end with attainable tasks resulting in success that can be celebrated.

We all find reward in successful interactions and activities. If a child is experiencing difficulty with remembering auditory information, consider adding in visual and tactile cues. In our daily routines, this might include incorporating music into auditory directions, using gestures or other agreed-upon hand signals, tactile cues (lightly touching a student's desk), proximity, or using an agreed-upon keyword. It is important to recognize that while initially multiple supports may be needed for the development of the auditory system, these can be slowly and intentionally removed as the auditory system develops and strengthens.

Auditory organization

Auditory organization is the ability to use oral and auditory information effectively and efficiently in a structured and organized manner. Sounds easy, right? Well, in fact, auditory organization offers complexity to the auditory processing and effective use of auditory information. Let's consider how a child processes sounds heard in a simple word structure. A simple consonant-vowel-consonant structure, "cat", is composed of three distinct phonemes or speech sounds, "c", "a", "t". If the sounds are presented with no visual cues and you are asked to identify the word, what would your response be? Did you respond, "cat" easily? The efficiency and effectiveness in identifying the word based on the presented sounds is the result of auditory organization. You were able to hear the sounds, organize them in the order presented, and blend them to arrive at the word "cat". In cases of auditory organization deficit, the response may be "act" or "tac". The sounds are all present, but the ability to organize the auditory information is diminished.

Auditory Amplifier

Let's consider how the ability to organize auditory information impacts following directions. Just like with the organization of sounds to identify the presented word accurately, multistep directions are often presented in a specific order. Without the ability to organize the auditory information effectively and efficiently, a child may confuse the order of directions, omit a component of the direction, or in some cases begin with the last direction first.

Children with deficits in auditory organization will oftentimes operate in disorganized workspaces, lose assignments, or fail to submit completed assignments. Consider assignments that include ordered steps that must be followed.

How might the scenarios outlined result in frustration in a classroom setting? How might they impact a child's success? Consider the impact on academics, social interaction, motivation, and self-confidence.

Do you think children might demonstrate increased frustration, lack of motivation, decreased social interaction, or avoidance of assignments? Why? How might these behaviors be interpreted if there is not an understanding or awareness of the underlying cause of these behaviors?

As you consider the above questions, let's realize the significant positive impact we can have on supporting a child with auditory organization deficits beginning with the recognition that behaviors are communication. If we understand a child is communicating through these behaviors and if we can begin to support the organization of auditory information, imagine the impact on a young child's trajectory.

Bloom and Lahey (1978) provided the organization of language into three distinct areas, including form, content, and use. These three areas provide the foundation needed for effective and efficient communication. A child's language and auditory experiences and interactions during their early years provide an important foundation for developing future speech and language skills. As you recall from an earlier discussion in this book, children's auditory acuity may be within normal limits, but experience difficulty processing the information, which can result in a weaker language foundation. It is important to understand these areas of language and the way they impact communication. Language *form* includes the sounds and sound patterns of speech and language (phonology), word construction and the parts of words (morphology), and the necessary rules for combining words and sentences (syntax). Language *content* includes the meaning of words (semantics). Language *use* includes the context and social aspects of language interactions (pragmatics). Our daily communication and interactions may appear simple, but when we consider the complexity of language expression and comprehension and add the need to process auditory and language information into the organization and integration equation, it becomes easier to understand why deficits in these areas can negatively impact efficient and effective communication to varying degrees.

When discussing the impact of auditory organization on communication, we need to consider expressive and receptive language modalities. Both expressive and receptive language are important for ensuring effective and efficient communication. Language comprehension, also referred to as receptive language, is the ability to understand language. This language area includes pointing to pictures upon request, following single-step and multistep directions across various contexts, and understanding questions in daily activities. Additionally, reading comprehension is important for interacting with the world around us and learning new information. Language output, also referred to as expressive language, includes expressing ideas and emotions, expressing a variety of grammatically correct sentence structures, and developing an extensive vocabulary for communicating and interacting effectively. It is important to note that written expression is also a component of expressive language.

As we consider auditory organization, the organization of auditory input may be challenging, but we should also consider higher level auditory output disorganization. In some cases, a child has processed the auditory input but is unable to organize the output to express. Older children have described this frustration to us in the following way: all the information is in their head, but feels jumbled and all over the place, and it takes too long to try and organize the information to respond. Oftentimes, discussions have moved on, school content has shifted, or conversations with multiple communication partners are moving too quickly, resulting in some children with auditory organization deficits to appear quiet, not social, or not wanting friends.

Challenges with auditory output organization can also occur during oral responses to questions or written tasks. Oral and written language are expressive language skills, with written language being the most complex form of language expression. Written expression requires idea generation, organization of ideas, orthographic representation of the ideas, and adds additional complexity with grammar and punctuation.

Language Acquisition: The Early Years

Auditory integration

Accomplishing tasks requires connections within the brain between auditory centers and other areas of the brain. These connections are referred to as auditory integration. In order to effectively and efficiently move, talk, think, read, and process during our day, information is constantly being sent to different areas of the brain for coordination and execution of tasks.

Auditory Amplifier

Pause and consider ten tasks you have done so far today. Have you tied your shoes, eaten a meal, put on a coat, brushed your teeth, read a book, exercised, followed a direction, or talked with a friend? All of these activities required integration of various stimuli. Perhaps you integrated auditory and motor if you participated in an exercise class. When you tie your shoes, you integrate visual and motor. A conversation with a friend likely required auditory, motor, verbal, and visual integration. Our daily activities are complex and require integration. When integration is challenging, daily activities may become less efficient and effective.

In considering stimuli presented and the importance of integration, we need to consider auditory information that travels along the auditory nerve but is not sent to other parts of the brain. The lack of connection, resulting in diminished auditory

integration, may result in less effective and efficient completion of tasks. Let's consider the integrated activity of reading. It
seems simple, we look at a book, we read the words, and understand what we read. Sounds simple, right? If you have ever
walked alongside or observed a young child learning to read, it
can be exciting, but also begins to highlight all the components
that are encompassed in this task that appears simple on the
surface. In order to be an excellent reader, good integration is
needed between several centers of the brain, including auditory,
visual, and language. When there are poor connections between
these areas, reading challenges often are noticed. We encourage
you to pause for a moment and consider all the integration that
is taking place for you to read a page of this book. Before we
invited you to pause, had you considered the complexity? Now
imagine a child who experiences difficulty decoding the words
in a book. They are unable to read accurately with increased
speed. What if you had to sound out each word or look up the
definition of multiple words on the page to understand the
book's content?

We know reading can be impacted, but deficits in this area may
also result in challenges with auditory information presented in
the absence of visual information. Increased time may be needed
to process the auditory information and provide a response to
questions or follow multistep directions. Perhaps you notice a
young child who developed a strategy of watching peers and
waiting to see what they do and following. The inability to integrate also may increase the difficulty with changes in schedules
or with transitions because these tasks will require additional
integration of processing the differences in the routine or shifting
focus to a new activity. Multitasking may become a persistent
challenge because integration is often a key component of
managing multiple tasks at a time. In our work, we have often
observed children unable to integrate multiple components of
information resulting in responses of "I don't know, I don't get
it, or I have no idea." This has often been observed when auditory information is combined with visual information or active
hands-on learning. When we think about the multiple facets of
instruction and communication in our daily lives, we can easily

recognize how integration challenges have the potential to impact successful processing. Keep in mind that, in some cases, a child is successful with an activity or task in isolation but, when combined with additional integration, is unable to complete the task successfully. For example, a child may be able to easily and successfully use a pencil to draw a picture but is unable to listen to auditory information and write down the information. This often becomes apparent when taking notes from auditory information is required. For some children, the use of a writing tool is not an issue, but processing auditory information and then putting that auditory information into words on a piece of paper in an organized and complete way is challenging.

As we have mentioned multiple times in this book, developing and practicing auditory processing skills can be fun. It is important to find activities that are interesting and engaging to the child. When considering auditory integration, games that integrate multiple modalities with auditory information are beneficial. Swimming, dancing, gymnastics, juggling, throwing and catching a ball, listening and drawing, and listening and moving are all examples of integration activities. In fact, children with auditory processing deficits, specifically auditory integration may find some or all of these games and activities challenging. Frustration may grow the longer these activities continue. It is important to note these are fun ways to engage in practicing auditory processing skills and children practicing integration may find activities difficult, but as their skills improve, you will likely notice decreased difficulty, increased speed, and an improved willingness to engage.

Amblyaudia

Amblyaudia, asymmetrical processing of auditory information, is the result of one ear performing better than the other during auditory processing tasks (Momtaz et al., 2021; Moncrieff & Schmithorst, 2024). It is important to note that right ear dominance is expected during development, with auditory symmetry for both ears developing with maturation. Amblyaudia may result from auditory deprivation during critical periods of brain development. Although amblyaudia is a relatively new term to audiology, it is not a new problem.

If you recall from the anatomy review in Chapter 1 and Figure 1.3, the majority of auditory information received in the right ear will have a more direct pathway to the left hemisphere of the brain. The left ear has a longer pathway, arriving in the right hemisphere and crossing over, also known as decussating, to the left hemisphere for auditory, speech, and language processing. By 12 years of age, we expect both ears to be working symmetrically. It is most common for right ear dominance/left ear weakness; however, it is important to note that left ear dominance can occur. Additionally, some children will have a strong speech and language center in the right hemisphere, instead of the typical left hemisphere. When considering hearing acuity, there is typically equal acuity in both ears; however, processing is asymmetrical. This is particularly highlighted for dichotic listening, when two different stimuli are presented to both ears at the same time. Two ears are better than one and having the information from both ears results in increased speed, efficiency, and accuracy for processing auditory and language information. If one ear is required to do the majority or all of the auditory processing, increased fatigue and acoustic errors are more common.

In some cases, the right and left ears have equal difficulty processing sounds. Dichotic dysaudia is defined as a weakness with both ears transferring acoustic information to the correct area of the brain for processing. Individuals diagnosed with dichotic dysaudia may demonstrate strong processing when a task is monaural or only involving one ear. Complex or dichotic tasks result in diminished processing abilities. Dichotic dysaudia often results in difficulty with processing auditory information in the presence of background noise. Many environments in our daily routines involve background noise, including classrooms, lunchrooms, restaurants, and auditoriums.

Signs and symptoms of amblyaudia may include primarily listening with one ear when communicating on the telephone, preference for sitting with their stronger ear directly positioned toward the auditory signal, or when given one earbud to listen to music or audiobook will always choose the preferred ear and may demonstrate reluctance to switch to the weaker ear. Additionally, similar to the discussion related to difficulties with sound localization in Chapter 2, a child demonstrating amblyaudia may always look toward the right or left ear for sounds. When someone asks a question or comments, the child may appear to look around for a significant amount of time to locate the person talking. This results in asymmetrical processing ability with a stronger and weaker ear. Children with amblyaudia may demonstrate difficulty in the weaker ear on monaural (one ear only) tasks as well. Academically, they may experience difficulty when listening with background noise present, reading comprehension tasks, and following auditory directions.

It is important to note that ear preference doesn't necessarily mean a person has amblyaudia. Many of us have a preferred ear based on handedness or writing while listening on the phone or having one ear toward the person sitting beside you. However, if ear preference is observed and processing auditory information seems to be more challenging than for peers in the same environment, there may be a need for a referral for an auditory processing evaluation. It is important to recognize behavior and listen to information provided by the child. Children often are able to describe what they are experiencing, providing insight into areas of difficulty. Young children may report, when asked to listen with the other ear, that it "doesn't sound right" in the other ear or "it is harder to listen with that ear." If you try to switch ears with the phone or earbud, a child might immediately switch back to the preferred ear.

Ear strengthening strategies

- ◆ Consider preferential seating for a child to support processing auditory information.
- ◆ Dichotic listening tasks, including auditory information presented in both ears and the child repeats numbers, words, or phrases presented in the specified ear.
- ◆ Listen to music, audiobooks, talk radio with an earbud in the weaker ear only.
- ◆ Use the weaker ear when talking on the phone.

◆ Ask comprehension questions for audiobooks after listening with just the weaker ear, to determine how much information was understood.

◆ There are specific commercial programs designed to improve amblyaudia that can be recommended by an audiologist for remediation based on the results of a comprehensive auditory processing assessment and recommendations for individualized intervention.

Prosody

Prosody refers to the brain's ability to detect subtle changes in the auditory signal, including pitch and loudness.

Auditory Amplifier

How do pitch and loudness impact meaning? Read the following statements aloud. You can read them aloud to yourself or to a colleague.

The car is red.

The car is red?

The car is red!

What do you notice? What are the acoustic differences? Does your inflection change? What about the loudness used when reading each statement?

In some cases of deficits with processing auditory information, prosody isn't distinguished. Consider the impact of each of the statements above sounding the same. Perhaps if the question was processed as a statement, there wouldn't be a response to the question.

Without the ability to process the prosodic information, how would you know the differences in meaning of the phrases? The phrases are identical in words but have different meanings. Questions include inflection indicating the need for a response. The phrase with the exclamation likely includes a louder and more emphasized statement. If we consider a broad impact of misinterpreting or inability to interpret prosodic cues, reading is also impacted. Difficulty with interpretation of prosody may result in difficulty with sight words and the inability to identify the main idea of information read or heard.

What is the impact of prosodic cues in our daily interactions? How much of interpretation of the meaning of auditory information is dependent on the ability to process prosody? What misunderstandings might result during interactions if prosody is not effectively processed?

It is important to consider prosody because it serves an important role in communicating and interacting with others, including the use of prosody, but also the interpretation of prosodic cues. Children with auditory processing deficit may experience difficulty interpreting communicative intent. The impact of this deficit may result in missing auditory cues for understanding sarcasm, humor, or irony. This impact has the potential to negatively influence friendships, social interactions, and overall communication exchanges. Additionally, children with auditory prosody deficits may have a monotone voice when talking and reading. We need to consider the impact of this on a child's daily life. Often when working with children with auditory prosody deficits, the child may present as monotone and non-expressive. In beginning to engage in conversation with the child, it becomes apparent that although they have a significant amount of knowledge, they appear unmotivated. In some cases, they are highly verbal but lack clarity and depth to their context. In addition to these challenges, perhaps there is a lack of demonstrating emotions resulting in difficulties with peer interactions. Peers may interpret a lack of excitement about an invitation to join a team or join in a pizza party as not wanting to be friends.

Prosody strategies

◆ Using a keyboard or piano to help distinguish between pitches would be beneficial. Hearing the subtle differences between sounds may help with articulation and letter sound discrimination for reading and spelling.

- Using a keyboard or piano or piano app, play two very different sounds and ask child to hum the pattern back (match the pitch if possible). Try two sounds to start and build to three. Slower presentations with greater separation between notes on the keyboard makes the auditory task easier. Faster presentations with smaller separation between notes on the keyboard increases the difficulty of the task.
- Singing songs, listening to music without words, and "humming" or singing along are recommended.
- Using a keyboard, piano, or app, play two to three sounds and ask the child to repeat the pattern using the words "low" and "high." Teach or show your child where the "low" sounds are and the "high" sounds. During the training, make sure the child cannot see the keyboard (auditory task only). After they are successful at distinguishing two different sounds (farther apart on the keyboard, easier, the closer the keys, harder), attach words to the sounds in order. Low-high or high-high-low, pay attention to the order of the sounds and appropriate labeling. If words are too challenging, have the child hum the sounds and then, with success, start to use words to label the pattern.
- Use animated facial cues. Teach the child about emotions, that we may hear easily, anger, frustration, happiness, sadness, tired, by showing them facial and body language cues. Show them a "happy versus sad" face and have them guess the emotion. Add auditory cues to demonstrate how different the voice "sounds" with those emotions. Although they may not recognize the changes in pitch, they may recognize that difference in loudness with the emotions. Combining both auditory and visual cues may help support them in understanding communication.
- Music training, sometimes called ear training, is available for developing distinguishing musical tones/instruments. More complex ear training allows the musician to hear and identify how far apart the sounds are, a fifth, third, or octave; minor or major chord. A piano, trombone, and saxophone can all play the same note, but they sound different. Can you identify the instrument just from listening?

Summary

We have explored auditory processing areas, including possible signs and symptoms connected to deficits in these areas. As we considered each individual area, we realized the potential for challenges in learning and communicating when auditory processing weaknesses are present. It is important to identify the challenging area to identify effective strategies for supporting the strengthening of the auditory processing system. As we move into the final chapter of this book, we will explore the importance of supporting student independence as children grow and develop their auditory processing and language skills during preschool and early school years.

References

American Speech-Language-Hearing Association. (1993). *Definitions of communication disorders and variations* [Relevant Paper]. https://www.asha.org/policy/rp1993-00208/#:~:text=A%20language%20disorder%20is%20impaired,(pragmatics)%20in%20any%20combination

American Speech-Language-Hearing Association. (2005). *(Central) auditory processing disorders—The role of the audiologist* [Position statement]. https://www.asha.org/policy/rp1993-00208/#:~:text=A%20language%20disorder%20is%20impaired,(pragmatics)%20in%20any%20combination

Bloom, L., & Lahey, M. (1978). *Language development and language disorders* (Ser. Wiley series on communication disorders). Wiley.

Bonacina, S., Huang, S., White-Schwoch, T., Krizman, J., Nicol, T., & Kraus, N. (2021). Rhythm, reading, and sound processing in the brain in preschool children. *NPJ Science of Learning, 6*(1), 20.

Fitzpatrick, E. M., Jiawen, W., Janet, O., Flora, N., Isabelle, G., Andrée, D. S., & Doug, C. (2022). Parent-reported stress and child behavior for 4-year-old children with unilateral or mild bilateral hearing loss. *Journal of Deaf Studies and Deaf Education, 27*(2), 137–150.

Grothe, B., & Pecka, M. (2014). The natural history of sound localization in mammals–A story of neuronal inhibition. *Frontiers in Neural Circuits, 8*, 116.

Ji, H., Yu, X., Xiao, Z., Zhu, H., Liu, P., Lin, H., & Hong, Q. (2023). Features of cognitive ability and central auditory processing of preschool children with minimal and mild hearing loss. *Journal of Speech, Language, and Hearing Research*, *66*(5), 1867–1888.

Lewis, D. E., Valente, D. L., & Spalding, J. L. (2015). Effect of minimal/mild hearing loss on children's speech understanding in a simulated classroom. *Ear and Hearing*, *36*(1), 136–144.

Lieu, J. E., Karzon, R. K., Ead, B., & Tye-Murray, N. (2013). Do audiologic characteristics predict outcomes in children with unilateral hearing loss? *Otology & Neurotology*, *34*(9), 1703–1710.

Momtaz, S., Moncrieff, D., & Bidelman, G. M. (2021). Dichotic listening deficits in amblyaudia are characterized by aberrant neural oscillations in auditory cortex. *Clinical Neurophysiology: Official Journal of the International Federation of Clinical Neurophysiology*, *132*(9), 2152–2162.

Moncrieff, D., & Schmithorst, V. (2024). Behavioral and cortical activation changes in children following auditory training for dichotic deficits. *Brain Sciences*, *14*(2), 183.

Moore, D. R., Zobay, O., & Ferguson, M. A. (2020). Minimal and mild hearing loss in children: Association with auditory perception, cognition, and communication problems. *Ear and Hearing*, *41*(4), 720–732.

Moss, W. L., & Sheiffele, W. A. (1994). Can we differentially diagnose an attention deficit disorder without hyperactivity from a central auditory processing problem. *Child Psychiatry and Human Development*, *25*(2), 85–96.

Porter, H., Sladen, D. P., Ampah, S. B., Rothpletz, A., & Bess, F. H. (2013). Developmental outcomes in early school-age children with minimal hearing loss. *American Journal of Audiology*, *22*(2), 263–270.

Riccio, C. A., Hynd, G. W., Cohen, M. J., & Gonzalez, J. J. (1993). Neurological basis of attention deficit hyperactivity disorder. *Exceptional Children*, *60*(2), 118–124.

Talarico, M., Abdilla, G., Aliferis, M., Balazic, I., Giaprakis, I., Stefanakis, T., & Paolini, A. G. (2006). Effect of age and cognition on childhood speech in noise perception abilities. *Audiology and Neurotology*, *12*(1), 13–19.

Walker, E. A., Sapp, C., Dallapiazza, M., Spratford, M., McCreery, R. W., & Oleson, J. J. (2020). Language and reading outcomes in fourth-grade children with mild hearing loss compared to age-matched hearing peers. *Language, Speech, and Hearing Services in Schools*, *51*(1), 17–28.

5

Considerations for Educators to Build Student Independence

Auditory and Language Rich Environments

The early childhood years, with a focus on the critical birth to five years, provide us with the wonderful opportunity to share language and auditory learning moments with children in their natural environment. The world has so many wonderful language and auditory learning and interactive opportunities everywhere we go, including homes, grocery stores, playgrounds, classrooms, doctors' offices, and so many more. Pause for a moment and listen and look around your current environment. What opportunities are there to provide a young child with language and auditory experiences? Are there sounds that you might notice and model? Are there objects to label? Perhaps the child is older and beginning to identify onset and rime for rhyming words. If you are interacting with an infant, perhaps you are changing your inflection or singing a rhythmic song. These shared interactions build awareness, attention, and discrimination of auditory stimuli in a young child's environment.

We know that our social experiences have a foundation in communication and interactions with people, ideas, objects, and routines in our daily lives. Communication exchanges encompass verbal and nonverbal communicative behaviors to support effective, efficient, and functional interactions and communication

DOI: 10.4324/9781032647098-5

across contexts in our daily routines. If we pause for a moment to notice the significant amount of acoustic and language information available during these experiences, it can be both intriguing and overwhelming. When we consider young children and the opportunity that we have to support their auditory and language development during their early childhood years, it is exciting! The really fun part is that opportunities to talk, sing, read, and play with young children build nurturing bonds, encourage reciprocal interaction, and build the auditory and language foundation for future language, literacy, and interaction. It is likely that you are already engaging in these interactions with the young children in your life. What do you notice during these activities? Do they respond with verbal or nonverbal communication? Do you notice them focusing on auditory information? Do they turn to look at a sound or imitate the rhythm of a song even if they don't know all of the words? These fun, engaging, and nurturing activities are building the strength of the child's auditory and language foundation!

Let's pause for a moment and take inventory of the various ways you are already supporting the young learners in your life. Many times, these interactions occur without planning or strategic implementation. Children learn through play! When we interact with young children in their natural environment, facilitating auditory and language experiences during play, we are supporting children during the important early years of their development.

Auditory Amplifier

Consider the answers to the following questions. You can answer them independently, write the answers down, or discuss with colleagues. Remember that sometimes others identify strengths and opportunities that we may not recognize when considering the questions in isolation.

1. Take a moment to look around and identify at least three opportunities for early childhood auditory activities in your current environment. How might

you elicit these activities with a young child? Are you already doing these activities as part of interactions and play? Did you recognize that simply engaging with children through these activities is strengthening the auditory processing system for future learning and interaction?

2. Consider two auditory activities that you might enjoy when interacting with a young child that you hadn't considered prior to reading this book. How might these activities benefit a young child's auditory and language development? Will you try the activities? What do you predict you will notice?

Communication Breakdowns: Finding Clarity

There is no way to avoid communication breakdowns entirely. It is highly unlikely that anyone is able to confidently state they have never experienced a breakdown in communication. The authors of this book would be the first to admit that communication breakdowns have been a part of our lives, in both our work in the field of communication, but also as a part of our daily lives interacting with others, too many times to count. We have studied and worked in the fields of audiology and speech-language pathology collectively for decades, but still experience communication breakdowns because communicating is a complex process, encompassing auditory, language, and environmental components. Of course, there are varying degrees of communication breakdowns, but we have all likely experienced that moment of realizing that either our message was not interpreted accurately, or we misunderstood a message we received. Those moments can result in frustration, confusion, avoidance, and in some cases, difficulty determining how to repair the communication. It may be helpful to explore a situation you have experienced that resulted in a communication breakdown.

Auditory Amplifier

In considering a breakdown in communication, can you identify a time when you have experienced a miscommunication? Consider that specific situation and let's explore a few questions.

1. Was the communication partner familiar to you or were you interacting with someone you don't communicate with often? Was the communication partner a dual language learner? Was the communication partner using a rapid speech rate?
2. Were you communicating about a familiar or novel topic?
3. Was there background noise?
4. Was the communication with one communication partner or was there a small or large group?
5. What happened once there was a realization that a breakdown in communication had occurred?
6. Was there an attempt to repair the communication attempt or was the attempt abandoned? What was the result?

As we have explored in the chapters of this book, we know there are many factors that impact effective and efficient auditory and language interactions and experiences. The question also surfaces in this discussion about how we repair a communication exchange when there is a situation that is not effective in clearly and concisely communicating. Perhaps, when considering the situation you outlined in the **Auditory Amplifier**, you recognized that you abandoned the communication attempt or alternately, you might have requested or provided clarification, asked for or provided repetition, offered visual or written information to support the verbal communication, or restated the information one-on-one, instead of in a large group setting. Any and all of these repair strategies may offer the opportunity to change the trajectory of a communication breakdown, but how did you know to use these strategies? How did you recognize that there was a communication breakdown? Why did you feel empowered to embrace the communication breakdown and determine whether to abandon the attempt or focus on repairing with increased clarity. Scaffolding, self-advocacy, awareness, and confidence can all play a role in these situations. The exciting part about including this discussion is that we can begin supporting children in developing these strategies for communication breakdowns during the early years and in most cases, we continue to have many opportunities to learn and practice across the lifespan. Let's explore classroom strategies for identifying children who may have weaker auditory processing systems and consider opportunities for strategic scaffolding!

Scaffolding: Strategically Teaching and Learning

At the core of scaffolding is the goal of providing appropriate support to enhance learning and skill mastery. This sounds simple, but when working with young children it is important to consider the zone of proximal development (ZPD). The ZPD provides a basis of potential for development, not simply what a young child is able and unable to accomplish. The ZPD is the level between what a child can accomplish independently and what the child cannot accomplish, encompassing what a child can do with scaffolded guidance (Vygotsky, 1978). We know that working on skills a young child can already successfully and independently accomplish does not propel development forward. Alternately, working at a level that a child is unable to achieve even with assistance will not progress development. In working within a young child's ZPD, we work between these two levels, providing scaffolding to support the child in achieving the task. We can incorporate fun activities to practice and develop auditory processing skills. There are opportunities to practice auditory processing within daily routines and activities, including games and daily interactions. Table 5.1 provides examples of these auditory activities. It is important to remember that we process environmental information through multiple

TABLE 5.1 Auditory Activities to Develop Auditory Processing Skills

Auditory Processing Skill	Auditory Activity
Sound localization	Key finder • Use key fobs with multiple sounds and place them in different locations. Support the infant or child in localizing the origin of the sound by looking, pointing, or moving toward the sounds.
Auditory discrimination	Same/different • Present two acoustically different speech sounds or environmental sounds and ask the child to distinguish if they are the same or different.
Auditory figure-ground	Add background noise • Provide exposure to a variety of background noise sounds, including classical music, TV, radio, environmental noises, or restaurant noise.
Auditory memory	Step direction • Following direction games with single-step and multistep directions. • Provide single-step and multistep directions, including routine and nonroutine directions.
Auditory decoding	Speech rate • Practice decoding sounds, words, and sentences presented at different rates.
Auditory organization	Sequencing cards • Utilize sequencing cards to organize a story, recipe, or sequence presented with auditory-only information.
Auditory integration	• Tie shoes • Tell time • Bouncing/catching a ball • Listening and doing

sensory systems. We know that information is not received in a sequential way and that we aren't alerted prior to receiving this information to ensure our systems are ready to process and integrate information.

We can focus on working within a child's ZPD to develop auditory processing skills. Table 5.2 is not meant to be exhaustive

TABLE 5.2 Strategies for Scaffolding Auditory Processing Activities

Area of Auditory Processing	Strategy
Decoding	• Keyword extraction • Study buddy • Pre-teaching • Discrimination practice • Verbal rehearsal • Slower speaking rate *Table 5.3 provides additional explanations of decoding strategies
Tolerance fading memory	• Quiet location for work, quizzes, tests • Personal Frequency Modulation (FM) system or classroom FM system • Auditory memory games • Multimodal teaching, visual aids • Preferential seating
Integration	• Notetaker • Integration games (games combining directions that include concepts, such as colors and movement, juggling, dance, swimming, music lessons, gymnastics) • One modality at a time teaching
Organization, memory	• Learning to use a planner, lists, calendars • Multimodality teaching and learning • Visual cues • Minimize auditory fatigue

but offers some strategies for scaffolding to support success. Table 5.3 provides additional explanations and goals for the strategies outlined.

It is interesting to realize that when we focus on working within each individual child's ZPD, we will have the opportunity to utilize individually focused scaffolds that will support a young child in progressing their auditory and language development. Consistent monitoring of a child's progress to determine when and what type of scaffolds will lead to increased efficient and effective processing is significant. It is important to remember that our goal is to focus on increasing the child's independence and mastery of the knowledge and skills. It is important to continue to evaluate the need for each accommodation as skills develop because not all accommodations will be necessary for the long term. The goal is to develop independent learners and adults who reach their goals and potential.

TABLE 5.3 Strategy Explanation and Goals

Strategy	Explanation	Goal
Keyword extraction	• A teaching technique to help students identify and extract the more important word or phrase from a textbook, lecture, or notes. • Until auditory skills are improved, the child is taught how to write down keywords or highlight keywords, instead of trying to write down everything spoken or read every word.	• Identifying the most important information for learning/studying. • To help learn summarizing, topic themes and organization of material.
Study buddy	• A peer partner is assigned to the student with clear guidelines. • Develop a system that allows for questions regarding assignments, page numbers, directions, or key information from a peer to the student with auditory processing deficits. • For some children, developing appropriate boundaries will need some practice but can be very effective for reducing the need for repetition from the teacher and will reduce/alleviate communication breakdowns.	• Provide appropriate assistance for classroom activities and reduce the amount of teacher intervention. • As auditory processing skills develop, there may be a reduction in the need for additional support from a peer.
Pre-teaching	• Prior to a new subject being taught, the parent/guardian/family member/friend is provided with the subject and vocabulary words. • The person working with the child will explain the subject and new vocabulary words. • In the classroom, this will decrease the auditory demand for the child and should increase interest and understanding.	• Understanding new material presented in class with minimal misunderstanding.

Developing and Utilizing Self-Advocacy Skills

When we consider the important skills that begin to develop in the early years, we would be remiss if we didn't discuss self-advocacy related to communication. We have an important opportunity during a child's early years to develop self-advocacy skills to support interacting, learning, and engaging in a multitude of environments. We can play a key role in this development through modeling, supporting, and scaffolding with all young children.

If you regularly interact with children, you likely have heard the response "what" or "huh" to something you have said. Have you ever experienced the frustration of feeling like you now have to repeat the long list of things you already said? What if we utilize some of these opportunities to help young children develop skills for clarifying what they have heard and what they need repeated? Consider if you begin to encourage a child to ask for clarification by sharing back the components of a conversation or list of directions they did hear and process. Then we have the opportunity to coach and support them in identifying what they will need clarified. It can also help adults understand what tasks may require additional support to meet an individual child's needs. In fact, teaching children effective ways to advocate for the support needed instead of responding "what" or "huh" can help others identify and understand the possible areas of auditory processing difficulty.

Instead of saying "what," "huh," or exhibiting negative behaviors like frustration, giving up, or anger, children can learn how to self-advocate in a positive way demonstrating their desire to succeed, learn, and cooperate. Let's consider some examples of comments or questions children can be taught to say to self-advocate and connect them to the area of auditory processing that aligns with the need, outlined in Table 5.4.

As we explore examples of what a child may be experiencing based on the statements above, do you think any of these situations could be perceived as a child not listening, not cooperating, or avoiding tasks? Could these statements of self-advocacy change the perspective in these situations and provide an avenue for scaffolding and success? We begin to identify how auditory and language processing skills impact a child's ability to participate, interact, and effectively and functionally succeed in their environments.

TABLE 5.4 Auditory Processing and Self-Advocacy

Child's Statement	Area of Auditory Processing
I heard you say math book, but I don't know what page or which problems.	Auditory memory
I think you were talking about _____ but I didn't understand.	Decoding
Could I have the directions a different way (visual, hands-on learning, or written)?	Decoding, integration
There was too much noise for me to be confident that I understood. Could you please say the directions again?	Auditory figure-ground
The dog is red doesn't make sense, but I think that is what I heard. Could you please help me understand?	Decoding
I heard that I am supposed to get my reading book and take it home? I think I am missing what I am supposed to do with my book at home.	Auditory organization, auditory memory
Can I please move to a quieter place? I am having trouble understanding. I hear you talking about the tasks I am supposed to do, but I can't understand.	Auditory figure-ground
I am reading the words, but the story doesn't make sense to me. I don't know what is happening in the story. I am confused.	Tolerance fading memory
I cannot listen and write at the same time. If I'm writing, all I can focus on is writing. I stop "hearing."	Integration
Statements, questions, and exclamations all sound the same to me.	Prosody
I don't understand what you mean by "inflection" or reading with expression.	Prosody
It takes me so long to read the sentence that I forget what it was about.	Decoding, auditory memory
My brain hurts from listening so hard. I'm tired.	Decoding, auditory figure-ground, integration, fatigue
The teacher's voice isn't loud enough. Everything around me is just as loud.	Auditory figure-ground
I can hear just fine, but my ears don't work right. I have to ask people to repeat all the time.	Auditory figure-ground, decoding
I heard you but I have no idea what to do.	Integration, decoding
If I can't see you, I can't hear you.	Decoding

(Continued)

TABLE 5.4 (Continued)

Child's Statement	Area of Auditory Processing
This is stupid. I don't want to do it.	Avoidance
Can you please just show me what to do? Don't tell me. That doesn't work.	Integration, decoding
Yes, I can hear you talking, but it doesn't make sense. The words just get all jumbled in my head.	Organization
Tell them to be quiet. I can't think when they are making all that noise.	Auditory figure-ground
What is wrong with me? Why can they know what to do and I don't?	Frustration
I'm so tired. My head hurts from listening so hard.	Fatigue
I heard it, understood it, but cannot remember it or can't do it	Output organization
I didn't hear you	Decoding
I heard you but I don't understand.	Integration

Auditory and language processing difficulties may result in immediate or future impact on a child's self-confidence. Most of us would prefer to engage in activities we are successful with on a regular basis. We may choose to try more challenging activities, but let's consider how we might feel if the challenges were present in many or all of our daily interactions and communication. Consider some expected responses to this frustration and perceived lack of success. We have observed and heard many reports of a child withdrawing from social opportunities, experiencing difficulty making and keeping friends, acting out or avoiding activities, and verbalizing feelings of failure.

Many children and parents have expressed a sense of relief from simply realizing there is a reason for these challenges. We have observed many children begin to verbalize more, tell jokes, share their frustrations openly, and in the most wonderful moments, recognize auditory processing and language can improve and begin to share the progress they are experiencing. With increased auditory processing and language success often comes a growth in confidence, a willingness to attempt new tasks, a focus on socializing with friends. Let's pause to consider how what may seem like small changes on the surface can significantly impact a young child's daily interactions and communication. We have experienced wonderful moments with parents and children as we walk alongside them on a journey to improve auditory and language processing. Tears of hope and joy, laughter as a child tells or understands a joke, reading becomes an enjoyable activity, and new social connections explored are evidence of the impact of improved auditory processing skills.

As parents and children recognize the reason for difficulties with specific tasks, including a well-defined area of weakness, supporting the development of self-advocacy becomes important for the journey. The reality is that some children will continue to experience auditory and language processing challenges into adulthood and supporting the development of self-advocacy becomes a key factor in their success with difficult tasks. It is important to build an understanding of when and how to advocate and continue to emphasize that accommodations needed during the early childhood years may not be needed as a child's auditory and language processing skills develop and improve. Advocating for what is needed at specific times in an individual's life is important to understand. The goal is always the optimal level of independence an individual can achieve. Don't minimize progress, even if it seems small, because the boosts of progress can lead to increased motivation to strive for and achieve the next level of independence with auditory processing tasks.

We want to emphasize that while this book is intended to provide opportunities for ensuring all young children have rich auditory and language experiences during the early childhood years, we recognize that in some cases, assessment and intervention by professionals will be important to a child's progress. If you are a parent and you have concerns about your child's auditory or language skills, we encourage you to talk with your child's pediatrician and consider seeking an evaluation with professionals trained to evaluate and support a collaborative intervention plan. Depending on your concerns and your child's needs, you may seek an evaluation with an audiologist, but it is important to recognize that speech-language pathologists, occupational therapists, and physical therapists provide inter-disciplinary insight into assessment and intervention. As we consider effective communication, integration across systems, and sensory input, we value the collaborative expertise of our colleagues across many disciplines.

Learning and Motivation

We learn through daily engagement and interactions with the world around us. The early childhood years, infancy through age five, and expanding up to age eight years, are critical years for developing the foundation for future learning and development. We experience the world around us through our senses of sight, smell, touch, taste, and of course, hearing! Young children learn through play and interactions, providing a foundation for social interaction, language, and speech development. This early development progresses to reading, writing, literacy, and social development. Children benefit from a strong foundation built on strong, nurturing, and responsive interactions, consistent language and auditory learning opportunities, and engagement with literacy experiences.

We can begin to build a child's motivation for learning during these early years by providing fun, interactive, and responsive learning opportunities. Singing songs, talking during daily activities, sharing reading opportunities, and playing with young children are important ways to build language and auditory processing skills during the early years. Singing provides opportunities for language learning and also allows a young child to experiment with rhythm and pitch. Reading to a young child supports auditory comprehension and vocabulary development. Books during these early years offer contextual information for children as they are learning language through pictures, repetition, and shorter sentence structures. These early opportunities also offer exposure to print. Providing fun opportunities to interact with books, toys, and sounds often motivates a young child to engage, attempt more challenging tasks, and build confidence.

Oftentimes when talking with parents, children, or teachers, we hear that a child who is experiencing challenges with language or auditory processing is not motivated. On the surface that may appear to be true, but the decreased motivation may be the result of the inability to successfully complete tasks, enjoy social interactions, or engage in auditory or language activities without fatigue. Generally speaking, we all want to be successful. What is the motivation if we don't find success and the result is feeling exhausted? Avoiding or abandoning situations resulting in these feelings is actually good problem-solving! When we take that perspective, it shifts the focus from a child who isn't motivated to a child who needs opportunities for success to build confidence and motivation. We are not suggesting there should never be challenging tasks. Practicing the tasks that are difficult is what will lead to progress; however, embedding the challenging tasks within easier tasks with less auditory processing can provide a better approach to practice opportunities and learning. As a child experiences success, we often see improved motivation. Recognize and share with the child when you observe success with a difficult task. Implementing these scaffolded and supported opportunities into challenging activities and interactions can provide a springboard for a child to realize renewed motivation and a goal of increased independence.

Summary

In closing, this book has allowed us to travel on a journey exploring the auditory system, including acuity and processing, which impacts communication, learning, and interactions. The importance of identifying auditory strengths and weaknesses can provide an avenue for utilizing areas of strength to enhance communication, while a targeted focus on areas of weakness can strengthen the overall auditory system. The authors of this book have seen the strength of children and their parents as they navigate auditory processing and language deficits and disorders. Our work with these amazing, hardworking, determined, and insightful children and parents helped us begin to explore the importance of providing opportunities for developing and strengthening the auditory and language systems during the early childhood years to positively impact ongoing learning, communication, and interactions as a young child continues to learn and grow. This book isn't written to provide all the answers but hopefully has offered a glimpse into the complexity of the auditory system and the connection to communication, literacy, and learning. Perhaps this book resonated with you because you can relate to hearing acuity or auditory processing or language challenges personally or with someone you know. Perhaps you know a young child who experiences challenges with processing auditory or language information. For some readers, maybe you read something that resulted in identifying ways to support a young child's auditory processing and language development during the early years with the introduction of new activities or through new scaffolds to support a child in achieving mastery of new auditory or language skills. Regardless of your reason for picking up this book, we hope you found something that resonated with you, sparked your interest in a specific auditory processing or language area, or inspired you to explore more information. Our opportunities to work with children experiencing auditory and language processing deficits and disorders will continue to inspire us to learn more and explore ways to support early auditory and language development so that each individual child can experience their optimal ability to learn and thrive.

Reference

Vygotsky, L. S. (1978). *Mind in society: The development of higher psychological processes.* Harvard University Press.

For Product Safety Concerns and Information please contact our EU
representative GPSR@taylorandfrancis.com
Taylor & Francis Verlag GmbH, Kaufingerstraße 24, 80331 München, Germany

www.ingramcontent.com/pod-product-compliance
Lightning Source LLC
Chambersburg PA
CBHW062037270326
41929CB00014B/2465